A Cancer Story:

Along the Road to Death by Metastasized Malignant Melanoma

Edited by Harold A. Geller

For Milli,

To life with no cancer,

Best Wishes,

Harold A. Geller

© 2012 Harold A. Geller. All rights reserved.
ISBN 978-1-300-57229-9

Table of Contents

	Page
Preface	5
The Saga Begins	7
The Cancer Spreads	9
Stuyvesant High School Commencement Address	15
The Saga Continues	19
The Biochemical Treatment Fails and The Cancer Spreads Even More	21
The Birthday Party	33
Richard Geller's 65th Birthday Song	55
The Last Days of Life	57

Preface

"Ne fuestra vixesse videar." It is said that these were the last words of the famed astronomer Tycho Brahe on his death bed. Roughly translated, Tycho's statement means let me not have lived in vain. I do not believe that my brother, Richard B. Geller lived in vain, but I do believe that telling the story of the last days of his life focused on his battle with metastasized malignant melanoma, may help others face a similar fate. The following treatise is a compilation of electronic mail messages, vignettes about my brother compiled for his 65th birthday party, and status reports from his beloved wife Barbara Bringardner Geller shared with me between the times my brother learned of his melanoma, to the day he died from the metastasized malignant melanoma. I am hoping that this rag tagged compilation will help others in their battle with cancer, and allow me to share with them a valued life.

My brother was not a rich man. Today it seems that a person's value is equated with the value of their possessions. Recently on television I heard that in a survey taken of online dating participants, the number one consideration about a date was their credit rating. How sad.

My brother was a mathematics teacher for 43 years, the last 30 of which was spent at New York City's Stuyvesant High School. He was for all those years a public servant, that is, a public employee. He was also a union member for all those years, something looked down upon in today's for-profit corporatized world. My brother was also a tutor and a taxicab driver. As a teenager he marched in protest of prejudice with Dr. Martin Luther King, and he also marched against the War in Vietnam. You can see his reference to the Vietnam War in his commencement speech made to Stuyvesant High School in June of 2011 which I had to include as part of this story of his last days battling cancer.

Albert Einstein once said that "only a life lived for others is a life worth living." I think my brother lived up to that Einstein mantra. He lived to teach his students mathematics, and he lived for his wife, son, daughter and their families.

The Saga Begins

> Friday, December 24, 2010 10:12 AM

Dear all,

On Tuesday I will be operated on to take out a melanoma. Last Thursday I went for a skin checkup and the dermatologist found two moles that were suspicious. One turned out to be an atypical mole that has to be removed and is only on the surface of the skin. The other turned out to be a stage 2 melanoma (4 is the worst). Nine years ago I had a stage 1 melanoma cut out. The surgery for stage 2 is different because they want to check my lymph nodes to make sure the cancer hasn't reached the lymph system. Therefore on Tuesday I am having the melanoma cut out and one or two lymph nodes removed. I will be given general anesthesia and will hopefully be home by 6 PM (an all day ordeal). Hopefully, the melanoma hasn't spread.

Today I will be flying to Florida today to see Barbara's mother and Barbara (who has been with her mother for the past two weeks). Barbara and I were originally coming back on Tuesday, but now we will be coming back on Sunday (there is a possible snowstorm Monday) so I can be in NY for Tuesday's operation.

Happy Holidays to everyone.

Richard

> Tuesday, December 28, 2010 5:34 AM

We just pulled into the garage. Having to wait in the cash toll lanes didn't help with our finish time!

Richard and I did amazingly well considering all of my middle-of-the-night apprehension. We didn't hit snow of any significance until half way up the NJ turnpike. Even the snow was mostly plowed (for example, 2 out of 3 lanes). We did slow down a bit so lost some time but there was not much traffic which helped a lot.

Manhattan itself was the worst by far. The streets were piled with lots of snow but the roads we had to use were sort of passable. The local bars were hopping. The hardest section was the gas station at 10th

Avenue and 45th Street where we had to fill up before returning the car. I was sure we would get stuck but we didn't.

Richard did most of the driving. Every few hours, I took over for about 1 hour while he slept. I had trouble sleeping when Richard was driving but did get enough in to feel refreshed when it was my turn to drive.

I checked some flight statuses during our drive, and every flight that I checked going into NYC was cancelled. So, it turned out we made the right decision since driving was literally the only way to get to NYC tonight.

After all this effort, I was more than glad to hear that the doctor had not cancelled the surgery. Imagine that! She is only doing surgery on Tues this week, so that would have been quite frustrating.

Tomorrow, I will bring Richard to the hospital at 9:30 and pick him up at about 5PM

That is all for now.

Barbara

Tuesday, December 28, 2010 2:34 PM

I just got an update from Richard's surgical oncologist, Dr Karen Hiotis. She said there was no evidence of cancer in the seminal lymph nodes that were removed. She said a final report from the pathologists is due in a few days but they don't foresee any problem.

This is great news and means the cancer has not spread.

She said we can discuss newer methods for screening for melanoma for Richard in his post op appointment. This is very important since this cancer came out of no where. Richard is examined every 4 months and this cancer was not present at his prior exam.

Interesting that the doctor came up from Baltimore this morning especially to perform this surgery.

Richard is in the recovery room now. I just saw him.

From, A very relieved Barbara

The Cancer Spreads

> Saturday, April 2, 2011 7:38 AM

Rita,
I hope this message finds you well whenever you see it.
I wanted to let you know that last Tuesday Richard called me to tell me that he has been diagnosed with lung cancer. He first had a persistent cough, then had a chest x-ray, then a CT scan. One doctor believes that it has already metastasized, which if true, is not good. Richard is due to be biopsied the coming Wednesday, but he has already made an appointment to see a specialist at Sloan-Kettering the following week.

Richard is chaperoning a math competition today (Saturday 2 April 2011) so I am planning on driving up to New York City tomorrow to see him.

I thought it might be nice if Allan called Richard. He may not be bothered by Richard again, ever.

Regards,
Harold

> Monday, April 4, 2011 11:07 AM

Hi Harold:

How horrible, what terrible news. I am so sorry to hear this, poor Richard and Barbara. Have you seen them? How are they doing? Would it be okay for me to e-mail them?

I will pass the info to Allan. No guarantees what he will do. Hopefully he is willing to contact them.

Love,
Rita

> Wednesday, April 6, 2011 4:13 PM

They removed over 400cc of liquid from his lungs (more than one 12 oz soda can) this morning. They plan to run a cytology test on it.

Next, they took a lung biopsy using a long thin needle and local anesthesia. It took 5 passes to get any cells. The first 4 passes came back with no cells. Finally on the 5th try through his chest, they got something. (I was told normally it takes 3 passes to get any cells.)

Now Richard is resting. They will do a chest x-ray in 2 hours to make sure everything is ok in his lungs.

More later.

Barbara

Wednesday, April 13, 2011 11:20 AM

Re: Notes from Richard's appointment with Dr Pavlick,
I just found out that Richard has the BRAF gene mutation. This is great news and it opens up many treatment options.
Barbara

Friday May 20, 2011

Virginia Cancer Institute, Richmond, VA
Dr Joshua McFarlane, board certified in oncology and hematology
Susan More , Cancer Research Nurse Coordinator

Statistics:
Weight: 143.6 w/shoes
Temperature: 97.8
Blood pressure: 123/81
Pulse 85
Oxygen 98%

Physical:
- Dr McFarlane asked Richard about his disease symptoms and examined Richard.
- Tumors under the left armpit: Dr McFarlane commented that these were not biopsied but were probably melanoma tumors. He added that they were about 1 cm in size last month and were superficial and barely there now. He said this was a very good sign.

- Coughing: Richard reported that his coughing had improved significantly. Dr McFarlane said this was another good sign.
- Breathing: Dr McFarlane said Richard's lungs sounded good. I commented that his breathing seemed about the same and shallow to me. Dr McFarlane said there were probably spots taking space in Richard's lungs. He said he would expect this and the proof will be in the imaging which will not be done until next month. He added that Richard had good breathing and the sound in his lungs was good.
- Other: He also said Richard's heart and belly sounded good.

Side Effects:
- Rash: Richard said it started 3 weeks ago but doesn't bother him much, is not painful, and doesn't itch. In addition to using a lotion without fragrance, Sue recommended using 'utter cream' for the feet if his skin is dry since it is thick and works well there.
- Joint pain: Richard said the joint pain bothers him a lot. He said it also started about 3 weeks ago, first at right index finger, then to his right thumb, moving to heals, to soles of feet, to other hand joints, and to knees. Richard said Ibuprofen relieves the pain but he had been asked to only take it once a day since it is contraindicated with the experimental drug. Dr McFarlane added that it was only a relative contraindication meaning one should use judgment and avoid it except if needed. He said an absolute contraindication means the drug should never be taken with the experimental drug. Coumadin is an example of this type of drug. He said there was no proof of a negative impact of ibuprofen with PLX4032 even though it shares the same general pathway for metabolism. Later, Dr McFarland and Sue said that Richard could take ibuprofen as needed to relieve the joint pain up to a normal recommended dose, or 2 pills every 4-6 hours for pain. Sue added that it is fine for Richard to take ibuprofen, Tylenol and naproxen (Aleve) as needed. When I suggested that Richard does not take the drug at the same time as the PLX4032, Dr McFarlane said the half life of ibuprofen is about 6 hours so some is still in his system when he takes the PLX4032.
- Mouth Cold Sores: Richard explained that he has cold sores last week but said NYU had given him Magic Mouthwash (a prescription) which eliminated the pain right away and also reBalance an over-the-counter medicine that corrects the pH balance. When Dr McFarlane examined Richard he said he

saw no evidence of the cold sores any more except for the minor remains of a sore behind the lower lip.
- Fatigue: Richard said he was fatigued at a level of 4 on a scale of 10. He said he was not as fatigued now as he was before he started treatment.

Sue later commented that her experience with the side effects of targeted experimental drugs is that the body adjusts to the new medicine after about 2 months and the side effects become less pronounced. She said this was not generally the case with systemic chemotherapy when the symptoms become more pronounced over time.

Other:
- Blood work: Sue said Richard's CBC (complete blood count) was perfectly normal. The white blood counts and platelets were normal. She said the SGRT was slightly elevated indicating stress to the liver. She said this may be due to the Tylenol Richard is taking several times a day or the general level of stress. She said it was not indicative of cancer in the liver. She suggested that taking ibuprofen instead of Tylenol may correct this problem. She did not recommend aspirin for pain since it may cause bleeding. She added that for some people ibuprofen was helpful to reduce a low grade fever like Richard has.
- Shaking of the hands: Dr McFarlane examined Richard for other neurological problems and said everything seemed fine. He added that Richard's electrolytes were normal. He suggested that the shaking of the hand may be secondary to anxiety. He said Richard should not worry about this unless the symptom continues or become worse and then he should go to an emergency room.
- Concern about spinal MRI: Dr McFarlane said the drug was probably reducing the tumors in every part of Richard's body, including the spine. He said they would find out more with the CAT scan next month and he did not see any reason to subject Richard to another spinal MRI which is an uncomfortable 1 hour procedure. He said that Richard should keep an eye out for any symptoms involving loss of control below a certain point. If these occur, Richard should get an emergency evaluation at an emergency room.

Next Steps:
- Dr McFarland said Richard should stay on this drug until it fails. He added that an article in the New England Journal of Medicine indicated that many people have good responses for a significant duration. If and when the drug fails, another clinical trial is a good idea. He said melanoma is a very complex disease. He said many mutations are involved and each is contributory. He said PLX4032 targets one mutation but that is not the full story. He said it makes a lot of sense to start looking around now at other trials to see what would be an appropriate next drug. He specifically mentioned a trial of the BRAF inhibitor with an MEK inhibitor which he said is not available at Virginia Cancer Institute. Richard added that this is a GSK trial.
- Dr McFarlane said they expect PLX4032 to be approved by the FDA in September. Sue added that this is Virginia Cancer Institute's first trial with the PLX4032 drug and Richard is their first patient with it though another patient is awaiting BRAF confirmation.
- When Richard has the CAT scan next month (scheduled for Thursday June 16 in Richmond), Sue said they would also include a scan of the pelvis to look for "boney windows in the pelvis." This would help determine if the cancer was continuing to grow in the spinal area which was a concern in late April. She said this CAT scan could then be compared to the 4/17/11 CAT scan.

In general, Dr McFarlane said his impression is that the medicine is working. He said Richard has low grade side effects which are tolerable. He said he would not recommend a change in dosage based on these side effects.

June 2011
Stuyvesant High School
Commencement Address
By Richard B. Geller

Ms. Suri, Assistant Principals, my colleagues of the faculty, parents, guests, my family, and the Stuyvesant HS graduating class of 2011.

I would like to thank the graduating class for having chosen me as your faculty speaker. It is time for you to thank the entire staff of Stuyvesant High School for teaching you, guiding you, helping you during and after school, and writing your college recommendations. Will all my colleagues of the faculty and staff please stand up so that the graduating class and their parents can acknowledge us.

When the Senior President and Vice President told me that I was the chosen faculty speaker, I wondered, why me?

I have been teaching Math at Stuyvesant for 29 years and I was never chosen before. By the way 29 is a prime number, there are exactly 2 factors for 29, 1 and 29. Maybe I was chosen for the approximately 5 basketballs that I confiscated from students during your 4 years at Stuyvesant, or the 17 Frisbees I took away, or the 113 decks of playing cards, or the 257 cell phones I took away and brought to Ms. Damesek's office. In case you haven't figured it out, all of those numbers are prime numbers. Or maybe you wanted to hear me say one more time: Off the 4th floor; 1, 2 or 5, not 4.

No, I don't think so. I think that you heard 3 months ago that I have metastasized melanoma cancer in my lungs and that you either had me as a math teacher or heard of me and wanted to honor me for my passion for teaching math. I think you also respect me for requiring you to behave as adults and you rarely disappointed me.

Thank you for honoring me. Ten days ago I found out that the experimental drug that I am taking is working and that the melanoma cancer in my lungs has decreased. Even through all of this the best part of the day is teaching math.

I have been teaching math for 43 years (another prime number) and still love it. I got lucky. I found a career that I really love. If you have been in my math class you know that I love the beauty and logic of math and love teaching it.

When I was in high school, I never thought of being a teacher. I became a teacher to avoid fighting in the Vietnam War, a war I very much opposed. I had to teach in a junior high school that had students who were underprivileged to avoid being drafted. That junior high school is only 9 blocks from this theatre. I was not a very good teacher my first year and had problems controlling my classes. During subsequent years I got better at controlling classes and really enjoyed teaching students math.

In junior high school I became involved in the math team and enjoyed teaching advanced problem solving techniques to the team. The team members interacted with each other very well and many great friendships developed. Teams are special. The members of a team become like a family.

When I got to Stuyvesant in 1982, teams were important and doing well. The chess team and the debate teams were 1st in the state. The Boys fencing team won the city championship. In 1982 there were 22 sports teams. By the way, 22 is not a prime number. It is a composite number because there are more than two factors. It has 4 factors 1, 22, 2 and 11. You will be tested on this later.

Three decades later and here we are. Teams are now even more special at Stuyvesant HS. There are now 37 sports teams. This year the boys cross country, the boys swimming, the boys fencing, the girls swimming, and the girls golf teams all won city championships. In 1982, there were 9 students on the debate team. Now, under the leadership of Ms. Sheinman, there are 180 students on the speech and the debate. They won a 1st place in overall school sweepstakes at nearly every tournament they attended this year. I congratulate all those teams for a great year.

However, the best team at Stuyvesant High School is the math team. In 1982 there were 55 math team students. Now there are 241 students (a prime number). I was the head coach of the math team at Stuyvesant for over 20 years. Many of the students still are friends long after they left Stuyvesant. I know of at least one math team marriage. They live a few blocks from Stuyvesant and have 2 children. 2 is another prime number. In fact, it is the only even prime number. A few years ago Mr. Cocoros became the head coach. I am now an assistant coach.

This year the team came in first in the state competition, first in the 9th grade Continental Math League competition, 1st in the city in the Junior and Soph Frosh divisions. The senior teams were fantastic this year. For the first time ever the senior teams came in 1st and 2nd in the citywide fall competitions and 1st, 2nd and 3rd in the citywide spring competitions. Which proves that the math team is #1. This is a fraction of what this senior class has accomplished. During the year, this year's senior class had pajama day, Beach Day, video game character day, sweatpants day, hippie day, twin day, sports Jersey day, Stuyvesant spirit day, College apparel day, nerd day, and tie day. But I have one question. What happened to Math Day?

And of course we cannot forget that you the seniors of 2011 won Sing as juniors and then won Sing as seniors, a feat rarely accomplished by Stuyvesant senior classes. The senior class of 1983, my first year at Stuyvesant, also accomplished that.

You have accomplished a lot during your 4 years at Stuyvesant. This graduation ceremony should be very special to you. Many of the people around you will be lifelong friends. So enjoy your special day today.

I have been to many junior high school and high school graduations as a teacher and even my own graduations. However, the most important graduations for me were my children's graduations. That is because for me, my family is #1. Yes, I am a parent of a son and a daughter (teachers do it too you know). Only when I attended my own children's' graduations did I realize how special parents find graduation. So give your parents a break today. Thank them for everything they have done for you. Let them take lots of pictures. Spend time with them. Let them enjoy it. Oh by the way my daughter graduated Stuyvesant in 1983. In fact, please stand up, face your parents and give them a round of applause.

I have some homework for you. Assignment # 1: Volunteer. Give back to your family. Give back to your community.

Tutor for free, help out at your church, synagogue or mosque. Volunteer to help a political candidate. Help your parents clean the house or apt, make dinner, babysit. Say thank you.

Give up your subway seat to someone who is elderly or disabled. Think of others. We tend to think only of ourselves too often. We should always be thoughtful and compassionate to others.

Assignment # 2: Find a career that you enjoy as much as I enjoy teaching math. You will spend at least one third of your life at work and it is important that you enjoy that part of the day. And that career doesn't have to do with math (the best subject, by the way). You will be much happier with your life if you enjoy your job. And if your parents don't like what you choose that is their problem, not yours. When they see you happy in your life and career, they will be happy for you too. My children decided not to go into math. However, they have found careers that they enjoy and I am thrilled and very proud of them.

I have loved being part of your 4 years at Stuyvesant. I have enjoyed watching you grow physically, mentally, and mathematically. Thank you for a great 4 years.

Enjoy college, find a rewarding career, remember to help others, and become the greatest and happiest senior class of Stuyvesant HS ever.

I leave you with the following words: **Math is # 1**

The Saga Continues

Wednesday July 13, 2011

New York University Medical Center
Dr Anna Pavlick, Principle Investigator
Caroline Sorlie, clinical research nurse

Statistics:
Weight: 146.3 w/shoes
Temperature: 98.7
Blood pressure: 119/75

Physical Exam and Side effects
Richard reported the following side effects:
- hair loss from the head and body (increased from last month)
  Dr Pavlick said patients rarely lose all of their hair. Caroline added that this side effect may diminish as treatment continues.
- joint pain (only in finger joints mostly right and right heal),
- skin rash (reduced from last month)
  Caroline said there is an over-the-counter drug that is helpful for rashes called Sarna(?). It is a topical steroid.
- fatigue (only minor but still need more sleep than before)
  Dr Pavlick said that more sleep is good for the immune system. It provides more down time.
- Sensitivity in the breast nipples
- No more coughing (a sign of reduced cancer in lungs and not a side effect)

Dr Pavlick listened to Richard's lungs and said they sounded very good. She said they sounded clear.

Blood work and EKG test
Both Dr Pavlick and Caroline said Richard's blood work looks good including liver function. I asked about the LDH level which was not tested but which Dr Pavlick then ordered. Caroline commented that it can be an indication of melanoma cancer activity but other things can effect it so it is not so dependable.

Dr Pavlick said the EKG looked good.

Trials at NYU
Richard is at the beginning of the 4th cycle of the Genentech expanded access study for the PLX4032 drug. Caroline said 6-7 people are signed up for the study of PLX4032 at NYU. She said they have one patient who has been on PLX4032 since the phase 2 trial and is still doing well on it. She said some patients do well for 14-15 months. She said NYU also had the Phase 2 and Phase 3 trials for PLX4032 with a total of over 30 patients. She said the current target for approval of PLX4032 is August but it would likely be delayed similar to the way Yervoy was delayed in getting FDA approval.

Caroline said they were doing the Phase 1 trial of the Genentech BRAF inhibitor with the MEK inhibitor. She said they had one patient on the trail and that patient was doing very well. I think I also heard they were doing the GSK trial with the BRAF and MEK inhibitors but I am not sure I got that right. Jean separately heard from Dr Flaherty that this GSK study has been closed.

Dermatologist exams
Caroline said all of their trial patients are required to use the NYU dermatologist, Dr Jennifer Stein, whose office is at their 1st Ave location. (She has Mon, Wed and Thurs appointments) Caroline said the study pays for all full body checks, biopsies, etc. She said this was appropriate because the drug results in all sorts of skin growths. She said the rate of these skin grows will slow down as treatment continues. Caroline said she would check to see if a pathology report or slides need to be sent to Genentech for the squameous cell biopsied over a month ago. Also, she said she would check to see if the study would pay for Richard's prior expenses with Dr Amy Lewis.

Next Steps
Richard will be given an appointment on Monday, Aug 8 for a total body check and for a CT scan, both of which are indicated by the study. His appointment with Dr Pavlick will be on Tuesday, Aug 9. (Dr Pavlick has Mon, Tues, and Wed appointments.) Caroline said they would try to schedule future appointments for after 3pm so Richard does not have to miss school.

The Biochemical Treatment Fails and The Cancer Spreads Even More

> Tuesday, August 9, 2011 11:44 PM

Hi All,

Richard had a new PET CT Scan yesterday and an appointment with Dr Pavlick at NYU today to discuss the results.

Unfortunately, the news was not good. Richard's cancer has spread to the abdominal cavity. Also the size of the pleural infusion in his right lung has slightly increased. The cancer in the rest of Richard's lungs, his liver and bone remains stable.

We are currently looking at options for the next treatment. These include a combo BRAF/MEK inhibitor trial from Genentech, a VEGEF pathway inhibitor from EISAI, and an immunotherapy trial for anti PD1 at Sloan Kettering. We will let you know as soon as we know more.

Attached is a detailed write up of the appointment we had with Dr Pavlick today.

Barbara

> Tuesday August 9, 2011

Richard met with Dr Anna Pavlick NYU and Caroline Sorlie, clinical research nurse.

Statistics:
Weight: 145.9 w/shoes
Temperature: 98.0
Blood pressure: 106/67
Pulse: 69

8/8/11 PET CT Scan
Dr Pavlich said that Richard's PET Scan showed new tumor implants in the abdominal cavity sitting on top of the intestine. She said these were mostly free floating and they probably spread through the blood

from another site. She said this new cancer probably did not contain the BRAF mutation and was an example of the cancer resisting the BRAF inhibitor. She said this cancer explains the slight pain Richard feels when he presses on his belly button.

Also, she said the pleural infusion in Richard's right lung was a little bigger. She added the other cancer sites including the bone were mostly stable.

Recommendation for future treatment
Dr Pavlick said Richard should start another treatment soon to address the new cancer growth. Her recommendation is:
 1. **BRIM 7**

> This is a phase 1 study which is open to patients who have taken the Genentech BRAF Inhibitor PLX4032 which Richard has been taking since mid-April. It is a combo treatment which continues the BRAF inhibitor and adds the Genentech MEK inhibitor. It is currently at dose level 3 which may end up being the maximum dose. Each cohort includes 3 patients distributed across the US. There is currently a waiting list for this drug. Richard was put on the waiting list yesterday when Dr Pavlick saw the results from Richard's PET scan. It is unclear when Richard could get on the trial but it will not be until the next cohort is started which will probably not be until Labor Day. The advantage of this trial is that it allows Richard to continue with the BRAF drug he is currently on and which could continue to control the sites where Richard's cancer is stable.

> In general, each cohort includes 3 patients who are treated for 6 weeks with a stable dosage. The toxicity is monitored during the 6 weeks. Subsequent cohorts increase the dosage and monitor the toxicity. If a patient experiences unacceptable toxicity, the patient is eliminated from the trial and the patient population for the trial is increased to 6 to see if the toxicity is experienced by a larger sample of patients. Dr Pavlick said GSK also has a BRAF/MEK combo trial but this trial is closed. Also, Richard would not be a candidate since he has not taken the GSK BRAF inhibitor.

> Dr Pavlick thinks this trial is probably the best option for Richard at this time because his cancer is aggressive and she would not like to see him go untreated for the 28 day waiting period required before most other trials can be started. Also, continuing the BRAF

inhibitor would continue to control the cancer that is currently stable.

Dr Pavlick said the one patient who is on the trial now at NYU has done very well. He was similar to Richard in that he had an aggressive cancer that bypassed the BRAF inhibitor drug. Since he has been on the combo trial, his cancer has stabilized and has responded again to treatment.

Claire Stein is the Clinical Trial Nurse at NYU for this trial.

2. EISAI 7080

This is another type of molecular targeted therapy that blocks blood supply at the VEGEF pathway. (I think I got this right.) This trial is open only to patients who have the BRAF mutation because they have experienced a better response than patients without the mutation. The drug is available from EISAI and was just started last week at NYU. Two patents have enrolled from NYU. Approximately 50 patients have taken this drug so far. Like PLX4032, it is a pill. The side effects include elevated blood pressure in 10-20% of patients, protein in the urine, etc. It is similar to the drug "Evastin" (sp?) which is used to treat breast cancer. It is now in expanded Phase 2.

Dr Pavlick thinks this is a good option for Richard but feels the 28 day waiting period is a problem because it would leave Richard untreated for 28 days.

Crystal Escano, is the Clinical Trial Nurse for this drug. She said they do not know how effective this drug is yet since NYU has very little experience with it.

3. Anti PD1 trial

This drug trial is available at Sloan Kettering and is a type of immune therapy. It is a small study in Phase 2 that may be closed. It has been going on for approximately 9 months. Dr Pavlick said she would check with Dr Wolchok at Sloan Kettering to see if Richard could be considered for this trial. Dr Pavlick said she likes this study for Richard because the responses are faster that those experienced with IPI (aka Yervoy).

Other treatments discussed but rejected
   1. **Yervoy**

Dr Pavlick said she would not consider this drug for Richard now since it takes 8-12 weeks for a patient to get a response to this drug. She said Richard's cancer is too aggressive to wait for this length of time. She said other patients she has seen at NYU who have come off of the BRAF inhibitor trial and have taken Yervoy have not had a good experience with it. She added that the side effects of this drug are not a concern for her since she has had a lot of experience with this drug and knows how to control the side effects.

   2. **Combo trial of Yervoy and BRAF inhibitor**

Richard would not be a candidate for these trials since he has already been treated with a BRAF inhibitor.
When I specifically asked about the Dana Farber/Harvard article published about the Rationale for Targeted Therapy + Immunotherapy, Dr Pavlick said these do not apply to patients who take the drugs serially: BRAF inhibitor followed by immunotherapy. She believes a combo treatment is probably more effective.

Next Steps
Dr Pavlick said she would call tomorrow (Wednesday)at about 6pm to see if we have any further questions and to let us know if she has found out any additional information. Until we make a decision, she suggested that Richard continue to take the PLX4032 drug.

Saturday, August 13, 2011 10:56 PM

Here is a quick update on what is going on.

Richard is probably in the phase 1 study for the BRAF/MEK combo trial at NYU. (He just has to pass a few prerequisite medical tests which he probably will be able to easily do.) In this trial, he would continue on the BRAF medicine he currently takes and then add the MEK inhibitor for 14 days out of every 28. The concept of this is similar to the drug he currently takes. The MEK inhibitor is intended to block the ability of the cancer cells to divide and grow at another point on the cell reproduction pathway. Richard will begin taking the MEK drug on Wednesday August 24. For one week before that, he will take a reduced dosage of the BRAF drug, as specified by the trial. We are hoping this combo trial will have similar results to what Richard had with the BRAF inhibitor alone but we really don't know. This combo treatment is very new and we have not found any data published about the response rates. Richard's doctor at NYU, however, has another patient similar to Richard on the trial and she said his disease has stabilized. We will hope for at least the same for Richard.

This Tuesday, Richard has an appointment at Dana Farber in Boston with Dr Stephen Hodi, a melanoma specialist who has published many, many papers on melanoma research. I made this appointment about 6 weeks ago and timed it to be right after Richard's scheduled PET scan so we would have up-to-date info to discuss with the doctor.

If Dr Hodi recommends something that he thinks may be better than the BRAF/MEK combo trial for Richard, then we will definitely consider it. Most of the other trials, however, require a 28 day waiting period without any treatment which would not be a good thing since Richard's cancer is quite aggressive. Also, I don't think it would be a good idea for Richard to be treated in Boston with a drug that has bad side effects since he would be so far from home. But, we are keeping an open mind to see what Dr Hodi has to say. He probably has a lot of information about what trials work well for patients like Richard and what trials don't work well.

So, we are leaving tomorrow morning to have a little vacation in Boston before the appointment. Richard made reservations at 3 good restaurants in Boston and we are staying at an historic little bed and breakfast in town. I will have my Blackberry with me so I will have access to e-mail. I will also bring my computer.

Barbara

Tuesday August 16, 2011

Richard met with Dr F Stephen Hodi (Melanoma Program), Dana Farber and Jennifer L Mikoll, P.A.-C, Physician's Assistant

Statistics:
Weight: 148 w/o shoes
Height: 5" 8 ¾"
Temperature: 98.0
Blood pressure: 125/85

Physical
The Physician's Assistant asked Richard a number of questions. Richard reported that he had no changes in bowel, no vision problems, no chest pressure, no back pain, no blood or mucus in the stool, no lower extremity cramping. Richard also reported a feeling of fullness sooner when eating and a feeling of bloating sometimes when eating. Richard also reported a dry cough recently.

When Dr Hodi asked additional questions, Richard reported that his appetite was OK, his energy level was so-so, his weight was the same and he experienced some shortness of breath when walking or climbing stairs. Richard added that he still bikes but it is more difficult.

Regarding PLX4032 symptoms, Richard reported continued joint pain in the hands and right heel, continued skin rash, and hair loss all over the body.

Both Dr Hodi and Jennifer did a quick physical checking Richard's lungs, heart and abdomen.

Treatment Options

Dr Hodi said the good news is that there is a lot of melanoma research going on. He added that we don't know yet how effective these drugs will be on actual patients and that continuing research trials are required. He said this was the golden age of melanoma research.

Treatment Options: Targeted Molecular Therapy

GDC Combo BRAF/MEK Inhibitor – Phase 1 trial
Dr Hodi said that MEK is on the pathway to cell division and is downstream from BRAF. If the cancer mutates around the BRAF block (which Richard's cancer has started to do), it will still need to go thru MEK to divide and grow. In theory, if the cancer can be blocked at MEK with a MEK inhibitor, it will not be able to divide and grow until it finds a way to mutate around this second block. He said the combo BRAF/MEK inhibitor is still in phase 1 trials and there is not much information yet about its effectiveness in patients. I added that the only information I have heard about the effectiveness of the GDC combo trial is from Dr Pavlick who said she has one patient on the trial who is doing well.

Dr Hodi said patients typically see a response to the MEK inhibitor in a matter of 2-3 weeks. So, Richard would know quickly if it is working.

I then asked Dr Hodi about a chart in his April 2011 article titled **Potential Therapeutic Strategies to Overcome Acquired Resistance to BRAF or MEK Inhibitors in BRAF Mutant Cancers**. He said the chart shows that patients who develop ERK dependent mechanisms to get around the BRAF inhibitor, are generally sensitive to BRAF + MEK inhibitors. He said this was generally true but added that we do not know if Richard has developed ERK Dependent or ERK Independent mechanisms, but most patients develop both.

Next, I showed Dr Hodi the diagram from another article he coauthored titled The **Future of BRAF Inhibitors**
http://www.dfhcc.harvard.edu/news/news/article/4124/334/?PHPSESSID=c84186b744715f955d507b9356d0f3b2
It contained a diagram showing "increased expression of antigenic proteins on the surface of tumors recognized by immune cells" on cells exposed to BRAF inhibitors. The diagram indicated patients exposed to BRAF inhibitors could be more successfully treated with immunotherapy drugs than patients not exposed to BRAF inhibitors. Dr Hodi said this was not confirmed in real patients. He said the reported rate of response is actually the same for both groups, i.e. about 20%.

I also showed him another statement from the same article stating "MEK inhibitors suppress immune function". He said again that was true in theory but he also has seen theoretical evidence of the reverse; i.e., evidence of increased immune system function with MEK inhibitors.

When I asked Dr Hodi about why the Phase 2 GSK Combo BRAF/MEK trial was closed, he said it was because it was full. He added that this trial was different from the GDC combo BRAF/MEK trial because the GSK trial excluded patients who have already taken a BRAF inhibitor.

PI3K inhibitor trials
When I asked about PI3K inhibitor trials, Dr Hodi said these are all very early trials with no information yet about effectiveness.

HSP Inhibitor
Dr Hodi explained that HSP is a protein that chaperones communications along the MAPK pathway allowing information to

pass to MEK where the cells are told to divide and grow. He said this inhibitor is even more experimental than the combo BRAF + MEK trial. He said they are opening a Phase 2 trial in about 2 weeks but said no one in phase 1 had prior exposure to the PLX4032 BRAF inhibitor Richard is currently taking.

Treatment Options: Immunotherapy

PD-1 anitbody (aka MDX-1106) trials
These trials use PD-1, a drug that blocks another antibody route of cellular signaling. He said a patient needs one prior therapy to be included in these trials but not IPI. A trial of PD-1 with prior IPI exposure will open in about 6 months.
He added that if a patient has underlying lung problems such as asthma, he may not be a candidate for this drug. He said Richard's lung problems are caused by the cancer and would not exclude him from this trial.

All PD-1 trials have a 28 day clean-out period with no treatment prior to getting into the trial.

PD-1 alone
There are two slots at Dana Farber for this trial. It is also available at Yale. There are 2 trials: one in Phase 1 dose finder and another in Phase 2. (I think I got this right?)

PD-1 + IPI Combo
This trial is still in early Phase 1 testing with a low dose of .3mg/kg.
BG Note: There are 2 ongoing trials in NYC offering anti PD-1, both at Sloan Kettering. One with anti-PD-1 alone (NCT00730639) under Dr Carvajal and other in combo with IPI (NCT01024231) under Dr Wolchok. The combo trial is in the very early stages of dose escalation with .3mg/kg. Both have a 28 day wash-out period prior to getting into the trial.

The PD-1 trials currently exclude anyone with prior immunotherapy exposure.

Combo IPI + Bev (NCT007790010)
The PA said that there were 7 spots left on this trial. Dr Hodi confirmed that there was a 28 day wash-out period before starting this drug. It is only now being offered in Boston. After examining Richard, Dr Hodi

said Richard would not be a candidate for this since his abdominal area is involved in the cancer and there may be risk of hemorrhaging.

IL2
Dr Hodi said there was a very low response rate for this drug. He said 15% respond, 5% have a complete response of which only ½ of the 5% are durable. He called it a roll the dice drug. He said it was not a question of whether Richard would get sick from the drug. He would get sick and it would require a hospital stay. He added that Richard was probably a good candidate for this drug since he was generally in good health, though Dr Hodi would recommend IPI instead.

IPI
Dr Hodi said that IPI has a 20% response rate. He added that it could take up to 20 weeks for this drug to work.

Adaptive Immunotherapy
I asked Dr Hodi about a new technique reported on the Dana Farber web site that 'educates' anti-tumor T cells to endure in cancer patients without the use of supplemental treatments that can often have harsh side effects. The procedure reduces T-cell death in patients. Dr Hodi said that study was currently closed at Dana Farber but it was being offered at MD Anderson in Houston and at the National Cancer Institute in Maryland. He said the process involves surgically removing a large chunk of tumor, growing them in the test tube adding chemicals, and injecting them back into the body. He said for ½ the patients, they could not successfully extract the cells, for ½ of those remaining, they could not re-inject the cells successfully. He added that the process was similar to bone marrow treatments.

Recommendation
For his next drug, Dr Hodi said Richard should take either:
- an immunotherapy drug now (IPI alone, IPI + PD-1 combo, or PD-1 alone)

- or the BRAF + MEK combo.

He added that there is a 'window of opportunity' for Richard to get onto the BRAF/MEK combo trial and it may not be available later. Dr Hodi said he does not have this trial and there are very few patients on the trial now but they expect to get it later. He suggested that Richard should pursue it.

Dr Hodi said there is a lot of debate now about what treatment to recommend for new melanoma cancer patient who have the BRAF mutation. He said some feel they should receive IPI alone or in combination with another drug. Others feel the patient should be given a BRAF inhibitor.

When I asked about a combination of BRAF + IPI, Dr Hodi said he was working on starting that trial but development is still in the early stages and it might take some time. I said that when GDC's BRAF Inhibitor is FDA approved, a patient could take it in combination with IPI, another FDA approved drug. Dr Hodi said he would not recommend this since there was no way to know how the two drugs would react when they are combined. It requires extensive testing including phase 1, 2 and 3 trials.

He added that when one is combining drugs, one must balance safety and effectiveness.

Conclusion
Richard will get on the BRAF/MEK combo trial offered at NYU. His first dose of MEK is scheduled for Wednesday, August 24.

Other
When we arrived at Dana Faber, Richard was asked to sign up for Ongomap, a program introduced this week at Dana Faber which takes blood, cheek swabs, and other genetic material (e.g. pathology slides) and runs it through a process looking for mutations. Richard signed up for this. Dr Hodi said Dana Farber would contact Richard if they need more material from him in addition to the pathology slides that they currently have. The PA said results of this would be available in 2-3 weeks.

As we left, Dr Hodi said we could contact him with questions, even though he understands Richard is not now his patient. He gave us both a card with his e-mail address.

I asked about Dr Friedlander who co-wrote some important articles with Dr Hodi about melanoma research. Dr Hodi said Dr Friedlander transferred to NYC because he was raised in NY and has family here. He said he has 4 children and was offered a good position at Mt Sinai, was still in melanoma research and would probably be starting some trials at Mt Sinai. Dr Hodi said he was a valuable contributor at Dana Farber.

Dr Hodi said he was a Yankees fan. He said he was brought up in Boston but went to school in NYC where he got caught up in the Yankees. He added that his father was born in Queens and was a Yankees, Rangers and Giants fan.

Photograph by Harold Geller

Photograph by Harold Geller

The Birthday Party, Saturday August 20, 2011
Vignettes out of the Life of Richard B. Geller

Mail Call
By Harold A. Geller

When I was five years old, I don't know what obsessive compulsion possessed me, but I always loved to get the mail as soon as the mailman pushed the mail through the mail slot in our door at 4513 Flatlands Avenue, in Brooklyn, New York. Hey, I even remember our telephone number on Flatlands Avenue, it was Esplanade 7-2009. Anyhow, one day, I was in my room upstairs and heard the mailman push the mail through the door. I ran down the stairs to find my oldest brother Richard picking up the mail. He teased me that he had gotten the mail before me. I was so pissed off that I just let go with a punch to his stomach. Richard was about thirteen years old then and even though I was much younger, I apparently had enough of a punch to have him double over and in tears. Our mom had been in the kitchen and was yelling "what's going on?" I was so afraid that I had hurt Richard and that my mom would spank me, that I ran upstairs to my room. My mom did come up and scold me for punching Richard, but I was never spanked. I was just told never to hit Richard so hard again. And I don't believe that I ever did.

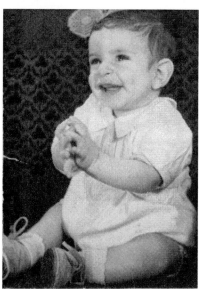

Photograph by Morris Geller

Look What I Found
By Harold A. Geller

When Richard was attending Brooklyn College, he was often out of the house and for long periods of time. I had often gotten into trouble going through Richard's books in his bookcase when I was younger, but with him gone so much, supposedly studying at Brooklyn College, although I wondered what he was really up to at the college, or if he really was at college as much as he was supposed to be. Anyhow, one day while going through Richard's desk drawers, I discovered copies of Playboy magazine. Well, I wasn't going to pass up an opportunity like that. I was pubescent so I used those Playboy magazines exactly for what you would think any pubescent boy would. I don't know if Richard ever caught on, but for a couple of years I would keep my eyes open for another issue of Playboy magazine that Richard would hide in his desk drawers.

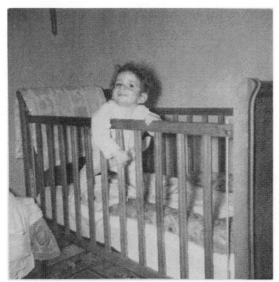

Photograph by Morris Geller

Richard Turns Fifty
By Barbara Bringardner Geller

When I was finalizing a surprise 50th birthday party for Richard many years ago, he told me quite directly that if I was planning a surprise party for him, he did not want it and he would walk out. I finally had to fess up and I told him a party was happening in two days and that he could either come and enjoy himself, or I would call everyone up and disinvite them. I gave Richard 24 hours to decide. He made the right choice and even enjoyed himself at the party.

Photograph by Morris Geller

Bouley'N Algebra
By Barbara Bringardner Geller

As many of you may know, Richard has a long history going back with Bouley Restaurant, but what many of you don't know is that much of that history also intersects with math. For example, 17 years ago when the Stuyvesant Math Team was growing fast and becoming more popular with students, Richard needed to come up with additional names for the many junior teams. He could have named them Team A, Team B, Team C, etc. But no, Richard wanted something more interesting, so he decided to name them Team B, Team O, Team U, Team L, Team E, and Team Y. Get it, it spells Bouley! This also got Richard the added advantage of an 'in' with the chef.

Whenever we had a meal at Bouley that year, Richard would send the math team results back to the chef for the B, O, U, L, E, and Y teams. Of course, the B Team came in first in the city. As an expression of interest, David Bouley suggested that Richard may want to have the team come for lunch sometime. David said the fall harvest season would be a good time since they get extra produce from the market and could make a nice lunch at a reasonable price. That was all that was needed. Richard set a date and invited 23 of the top students and the principal, Murray Kahn. One of the students was Alex Khazanov who was the top 1994 high school student in the USA and one of the members of the famous 1994 US Math Olympiad Team which attained a perfect score in the international competition.

David Bouley himself came up with a special Stuyvesant Math Team menu printed on parchment, pressed with dried flowers, and placed at the tables of the participants. Richard made sure that all the top students came and paid for those who could not afford it. He also insisted that the students dress properly for the occasion and brought extra jackets from the closet of his son Jason for anyone who didn't have one and also several ties and even an extra pair of shoes.

And a great meal it was. The students still talk about it, especially the assorted sorbets and the famous Bouley hot chocolate soufflé for dessert.

Scare Off Those Cancer Cells
By Barbara Bringardner Geller

Patty Johann is a good friend of ours and is a mathematics professor in Glascow, Scotland. She just loves to recount Richard's advice to her about how to prevent her students from cheating. She was particularly impressed with the authoritative voice and demeanor he would use to announce to his high school students that no cheating would be allowed, ever!

When Patty heard that Richard had cancer, she said: "If anyone can get well by sheer force of will, it is Richard. I keep imagining him walking into a classroom full of cancer cells, putting on his ultra-scary face, and pounding on the desk, all while he announces that they will NOT CHEAT [him of his health]! The next image my overactive imagination conjures up is, of course, of the cells being scared out of their wits, jumping out of their metaphorical skins, and then slinking off with their metaphorical tails between their legs. I know I'd be scared!"

Are You Sitting Down?
By Mikiko Kaneko

Back in June of 1997, Jason and Mikiko were married just three weeks after having first met. They just did it without telling anybody about it. It was very hard for both of them to tell their families. When Jason called his dad, Richard, from Japan, he asked: "Are you sitting down? I have big news to tell you." Then Jason told his dad that he had already gotten married a few days earlier. Richard was not angry as Jason thought he might have been. Instead Richard said, "Wow, that's great news. You made my week!"

Photograph by Harold Geller

A City Clerk Wedding
By Robert Bringardner

The wedding of Barbara and Richard took place on a cold day in February 1983. It was unlike any other event that I have ever attended. No expense was spared, at least for the wedding-related activities, especially the magnificent dinner at Lutece. I would hate to know how much that cost! However, the wedding ceremony itself was a different story.

I have never attended a wedding ceremony at the City Clerk's office in City Hall before, but I gather that they are usually very small affairs. As described on the current City Clerk web site, you just pay $25 for your license, wait at least 24 hours, and then show up during regular business hours with a witness. No reservations or appointments are accepted. That is not the way their wedding went down.

The entourage was guided to City Hall by various means of public transportation. As we all walked into the room for the ceremony, the Clerk was visibly annoyed. I wish I could convey his facial expression or remember exactly what he said. He was very unhappy that these people were taking up so much of his time. For most engaged couples, it would have ruined the entire wedding but it had absolutely no effect on Richard and Barbara. They were all dressed up. Many of their friends and family were present as witnesses, and they were going to enjoy the memorable occasion! And everyone did, except for the Clerk who probably got home five minutes later than he had planned that day.

Photographs by Robert Bringardner

"Ricky's" Students
By Barry Feldman

When my daughter, Stacy, was not quite 2 years old, she just wasn't able to say "Richie." It would always come out "Ricky." Well, I remember one time when she called him "Ricky" and he said, rather sternly, to a two-year old mind you: "My name is Richard, not Ricky." Stacy, being the very polite child that she was, said, "Okay, Ricky."

No story about Richard could be complete without some comments made by Richie's Stuyvesant students. There are a number of these, acquired over the years, on a web site about rating teachers. Most of the comments are favorable. The one I like the most, however, is this one: "He made a girl in my class cry for touching his newspaper." I told Richie about this comment and he said, "Well, she shouldn't have touched my newspaper!" I thought it was funny, but I have a warped sense of humor.

Here are some of the other comments from the Rate My Teacher webpages:
- Best math teacher ever!
- A bit scary, but a great teacher.
- Very, very tough. He's a great man, you'll have to really work to get a good grade
- You'll definitely learn, just don't expect an easy grade.
- Very intimidating, but amazing teacher.
- Best math teacher ever. He might be really strict and grades pretty harshly, but he actually cares about his students so much and I have so much respect for him.
- Great teacher! If you don't understand something, go to his help class. Before a test on Thursday, he offers help on Wednesday after school. Math is #1, lol and he makes math enjoyable and fun.
- He's somewhat terrifying and his tests made me cry. But he offers tutoring if you need it, legitimately cares about his students, and is a lot nicer outside of the classroom.
- I love him. His notes are so helpful you actually don't have to teach yourself from the textbook. Downside: he is such a good teacher that when you get a different one you'll start failing, like I am.
- Not the nicest teacher when it comes to grades but he is amazingly good. You may hate him early but he's totally

worth it. He's really good and genuinely very nice overall and pretty amusing.
- Great teacher; easily one of the best at Stuy. Unlike most math classes, in his class you actually are taught the material, rather than being expected to look it up in the textbook and teach yourself.
- A great man who knows how to teach. He's a good person with a great heart who treats each student like his own child. Just work hard and study and you will do good. I never learned more math from ne1 else
- I had Mr. Geller in 1974 - 1976, at J.H.S. 143. More than 30 years later, I can tell you he had a great impact in my education and that of my classmates. He is one of the best you'll ever meet. I hope life is good to him.

Photograph courtesy of Barry Feldman

War Cry Origins
By Barry Feldman

When Richie was still at the first school he taught at, Junior High School 143, he had a problem with the Music Department. Actually, all of the math teachers who taught classes that had to take New York State Regents examinations had the same problem; that is, the band, orchestra, and vocal talent teachers were pulling their students out of several subjects each day because of upcoming concerts. As a result, it was impossible to teach new lessons to the remaining students because too many were missing. Richie forbid his students from going to these extra music rehearsals and boisterously screamed, "Math is #1!" This became his signature outburst whenever a student asked to be excused from math class for any reason whatsoever. And to this day, Richard still proclaims with reverence, "Math is and always will be, Numero Uno!"

Everyone's Biggest Fan: Sports or Math – What is really #1?
By Sue Bringardner Kennedy

Richard has always been a big sports fan. At no time was this more apparent than when he and Barbara would make the trek to a niece's or a nephew's athletic competition. This is difficult for him, because even though he loves sports, with Richard, math is always #1. How to serve both masters? He deals with this by toting his man purse to the games, which is disguises as a plastic shopping bag. This is often filled with math problems or math competition work. During lulls in the action, or when a niece or nephew is "riding the pine," he is hard at work on a math problem. As an added bonus of his attendance, with Richard's help, Barbara has gotten an important baseball tip: she has learned the difference between a hit and hitting into a double play!

What is Really #1: Part II
Even though Richard jokes about math being #1, this is a tough competition. In addition to math, there are the aforementioned sports, fine food and wine, and biking all competing for this honor. However, we all know from his behavior that family is really #1 for him.

A Gourmet Meal?
By Sue Bringardner Kennedy

Everyone knows how Richard famously enjoys fine food and wine. When he comes to Delaware, he accommodates the locals, and Barbara too, by going out to dinner with us to the local cheese steak place, "Charcoal Pit," even though he complains about how expensive it is! At other times, when he cooks for us, it is always a gourmet meal. As a matter of fact, the inspiration he has provided over these many years is an unappreciated reason why the Thanksgiving meals we share with the Gellers always win the "Thanksgiving Championship."

Attentive Uncle and Nanny, Even with Infants and Toddlers
By Sue Bringardner Kennedy

Lots of uncles will relate to their nieces and nephews, but Richard has always shown great flexibility regardless of their ages. This started with his nearby presence at the birth of two of them, as a support for displaced older siblings. When our children were infants and toddlers, he was always willing to carry them around or follow them at a respectful distance as they walked around the block. He would play

"Big Trucks" with the big truck fans. As they got older, he would let them ride in his car, and he would watch his speed when they did, so that they could continue to get older. In middle childhood, he became their first employer and again showed flexibility by blending his two interests, getting them started on math team work, stuffing envelopes, etc., and showing a willingness to help them with math homework at ANY time. Funny, I don't think anybody has taken him up on this yet. Finally, as teenagers and young adults, he attends graduations and has always been willing to show them a good time if they came up to the "Big Apple."

Always There When You Need Him
By Sue Bringardner Kennedy

Richard is definitely a person you can count on. During our family's crisis, he was a regular, almost weekly presence, despite living more than 100 miles away and having a very busy life. In the eyes of our children, however, he and Barbara lived at the Christiana Hilton. Richard and Barbara probably felt more like they lived on the New Jersey Turnpike. Richard was always ready, willing, and able to do whatever he could do to help out.

A Graduation Dinner
By David and Jean Whitcomb

Richard was always at the big family events including those for his nieces Sarah and Emma. During a graduation celebration in Houston, we had some scheduling issues with arrivals, departures and the times of formal events. It turned out that there was very little overlap between Richard's and Sarah's time in Houston; but, we wanted to schedule Emma's graduation dinner to include everyone. Richard, always a thoughtful and careful person, was concerned that Sarah might miss her sister's graduation dinner if it were scheduled to include him, due to the possibility of a delayed flight. After consulting with Sarah we decided to take a chance and it turned out great. Hopefully, Richard was not too uncomfortable with this decision, but it was very important to Emma, Sarah and the rest of us, that he be included. Besides, if he had not been there, Emma would not have been able to enjoy wine from the top shelf of the restaurant, which was a gift from Richard!

The Finest and Most Expensive Restaurants
By David and Jean Whitcomb

We could always count on Richard to select the finest and most expensive restaurants in the area. However, without Richard we would never have experienced Rao's, Bouley, or Lutece; and, they really are the greatest restaurants. Even when we were together outside of New York, Richard knew where to go and where not to go. Fortunately, Richard could be flexible!

A Devoted Cheerleader
By Sarah Whitcomb

It was May 2008 in Madison, Wisconsin. Uncle Richard and Aunt Barbara flew to Madison to cheer me on as I ran my first marathon, and boy did they cheer. Aunt Barbara is no slouch when it comes to cheering, but Uncle Richard stood out as being an exceptionally vocal, devoted, and energetic cheerleader. He popped up at least a half dozen different places along the course and cheered with such vigor and distinction, that he lifted, not just my legs, but the legs of the runners around me. A few even told me that they were going to keep close to me to be sure and get as much of Uncle Richard's cheering energy as possible! That's my Uncle Richard, a devoted cheerleader.

Your Leadership is in Question
By Ken Rosenstein

One day, in the late 70's, or was it the early 80's, Richard, Barry and I, along with our wives decided to go to Lutece, as a way of celebrating a successful business cycle. Lutece was a very fine, upscale, expensive, five star restaurant. Richard and Barbara were regulars there and even had conversations with the world renowned Chef Andre (Soltner).

This was the first time that I had ever been to a restaurant of such caliber. My only knowledge of high-end dining was from what I had seen on television or in the movies. I put on my best Sunday clothes and of course brought along a wad of cash. I was anxiously anticipating the meal. I expected to have the time of my life and I wanted to experience it all. I must admit that once we were seated I was unnerved and intimidated by the surroundings. I was the proverbial "fish out of water."

Richard's menu had prices but our menus did not. It turns out that this was the normal procedure because the reservation was made in Richard's name. Furthermore, we were expected to order through Richard. Okay, I'm fine with those rules.

The very formal head waiter, elegantly dressed in a tuxedo, came to our table and we began to order. Richard began by ordering a Grande Marnier Soufflé, which is a dessert. You see, you must order this item at the beginning of the meal because it takes a long time to prepare. I said that I wanted the same thing, to which Richard said, "No!" I said, "Why not?" He told me that it was large and that we could share it. I responded to him by saying that I did not want to share, I wanted my own. As we continued to go back and forth, the head waiter restored law and order in the restaurant universe when he said in a very thick French accented English, "monsieur, your leadership is in question."

That was the end of it, Richard and I shared the soufflé and many years of a funny incident.

Richard and the Cell Phone
By David Linker

Richard and I were at a Math Team contest. His wife Barbara, called me on my cell phone to tell me that she had just been in an automobile accident. She didn't try calling Richard directly because she knew he doesn't keep his cell phone turned on. So Barbara asked me to find Richard and have him call her. I did find Richard and I relayed to him Barbara's message. He responded that he would call her immediately. And wouldn't you know the next thing he did was to ask if he could borrow my cell phone to call Barbara.

Photograph by Morris Geller

A Marzipan Banner
By Lora Kahn

I remember when I was the beneficiary of Richard's restaurant expertise. It was in the Spring of 1989 when I received my Ph.D. in English Literature from the City University of New York Graduate Center. Richard and Barbara invited me to a dinner at Lutèce to celebrate. It was truly a memorable evening for me. I remember that I had something with morel, mushrooms that I had never tasted before. But the best part of the meal for me was dessert. Richard and Barbara had arranged for a marzipan banner emblazoned with the icing message "Congratulations Dr. Kahn." At one point in the evening Andre Soltner came out to wish me well, and I felt like a celebrity. I kept the marzipan banner in my refrigerator long past its expiration date.

On A Bicycle Built For One
By Edwin Kahn

My most impressive memory of Richard was of him bicycling alongside of my bus, going north on Amsterdam Avenue one weekday afternoon. As I recall, there was considerable traffic at the time. I looked outside my window and there was Richard pedaling at a fast pace alongside of the bus. He and the bus were traveling at a similar speed for several blocks. I tried to get his attention through the window; however, I never did get his attention that day. The bus stopped and Richard kept on going.

On the Road to Gourmand
By Joan and Danny Cohen

It was fun helping Richard turn into a gourmand. We got to go to all the special restaurants in New York. Of course the most special of all was Lutece. Anyone who knows Richard knows that Lutece became a very special place for him, especially after he found out that Lisa was cancer-free.

All In the Family on Bicycle
By Alice Cohen

The one thing that will always stand out in my mind about Richard, is the time that he biked across Central Park to the hospital where my mother had emergency neurosurgery. There Richard was in his biking outfit telling the hospital staff that he was family. He then proceeded to talk to the doctor about bicycling. It helped all the Cohens get through a most difficult time. I will never forget that incident.

Photograph by Morris Geller

A Game Old Duck
By Jean Houvener and Sandy Smithson

We first met Richard a long, long time ago, back in the dark ages: Barbara and Richard were first dating. We invited them to join two other friends of ours for a Thanksgiving Day dinner. We had not as yet met Richard. He was actually working that day; driving a taxicab. We were shocked that Barbara was dating a cab driver. However, we soon learned that there was much, much more to him than just taxi driving. Richard stopped by long enough to have some turkey and other edibles. Having dinner with Barbara and four lesbians bothered him not at all – a real trooper.

Over the years Richard has attended many classical music concerts, perhaps not his favorite type of music. Jean has sung in many of these concerts, and if Barbara wants to go, they go. Sure, at times Richard appears to struggle to keep himself from falling asleep, for which we are grateful, and Jean very much appreciates his loyalty and support over the years.

Being a big city boy, Richard is not overly fond of being out in nature or in a garden. But he is a "game old duck" and when he comes to our garden, he takes a walk around to observe the garden. He has even been known to sit a spell in our "hidden garden" amongst the trees.

No compilation of anecdotes would be complete without many food references. We remember with pleasure verging on ecstasy, sauteed foi gras and pea soup a la Soltner, salads with fruit, lamb chops, and other delights of the palate. There have been so many lovely meals with Chez Geller, that it would be hard to recount them all.

The Most Memorable Dinner
By Susan Lichy

When we moved into our new apartment Richard and Barbara said they wanted to make us dinner as a house-warming gift. Of course we said "sure why not, that sounds like fun." Well, to our surprise it was a most exciting dinner. We each had a menu so we knew exactly what we were having. We started out with salads, then gazpacho. The feast continued with pasta garnished with basil and ricotta cheese, straight from Rao's cookbook. We also had sides of broccoli with a loin of lamb. To top it all off, we had a delicious dessert of berries and freshly whipped cream.

Richard included the kids in the dinner preparations, and while making the gazpacho I asked him to add a little more garlic. I guess Richard knows Barbara better than most spouses because he said Barbara would taste the extra garlic. Sure enough, when Barbara walked in Richard innocently said. "Taste the gazpacho honey" and she replied: "A little too garlicky." I was impressed by Barbara's refined taste buds but even more impressed by Richard's ability to predict Barbara's reaction. It was so much fun and by far the warmest house-warming gift we have ever had. Since then we have had many wonderful dinners with Barbara and Richard but that one was by far the most memorable dinner.

Good Shepherd, Good Sport
By Marilyn and Nick Geti

When our granddaughter, Kaila, was about two or three years old, we asked Richard and Barbara if they could go with Kaila and Marilyn to the Central Park Zoo while her parents went to see a play. Since we had become countrified and not used to the sole care of Kaila, this trip was rather intimidating. Richard shepherded Kaila and her grandmother through the many animal houses, eating food from the vendors, and watching the sidewalk shows. Richard had created a most memorable experience.

A more rigorous adventure for us, not so for Richard, was his shepherding us on the Five Borough Bike Tour. Nick and Richard wanted to do the official start in lower Manhattan while Marilyn and Barbara thought a less strenuous trip would be to join the route at Central Park. So off we all go. We first had to get on the subway. Nick was very dubious about taking bicycles on the subway. Richard assured Nick that it was a special event and that bringing bicycles on the subway was allowed. A couple of passengers were a little annoyed with Nick and wouldn't step aside so he could fit his bicycle onto the train. But he persisted and managed to clear the closing door just in time.

Once off the subway Nick and Richard had some distance to go. Richard rode like a madman, dodging cars as if he was driving a taxicab. It scared Nick since he had no intention of arguing with 3000 lbs of metal alongside of him. Richard laughed and kidded about getting used to New York traffic, otherwise they would never get to their destination on time. Nonetheless, at times he had to slow down and wait for Nick to catch up. Well, they made it on time and began their tour. A short while later Nick and Richard met Barbara and Marilyn in Central Park just where they had agreed to meet. It was no problem at all.

As we all neared the end of the 43 mile route, three of us were pretty dragged out and had to sit down before the final leg across the Verrazano Narrows Bridge. Our skin was raw from the bicycle seats, but Richard was still in good shape and riding circles around us. Richard was indeed the good shepherd and in general just a real good sport.

Richard's Artistic Side
By Janice Hanahan

Over the years, the most memorable occasions I recall with Richard always center on food. I still remember how much Richard enjoyed planning the wonderful feast at Lutece following his marriage to Barbara at City Hall. He took such pleasure in being a host to his friends and family on this occasion, providing them with great food and wine. Over the years, he and Barbara prepared many good meals at their apartment for me. Richard loved to serve such complex and delicious desserts! One scrumptious example is his raspberry soufflé. Then there are the great parties at Barbara's and Richard's. One of my favorite parties was one for Barbara's birthday, where Richard prepared a dazzling array of great dishes in honor of the love of his life. I also remember a meal at Bucks County, where Richard gave Lily a lesson in preparing and plating fish elegantly. The reason these occasions are so memorable is not the food, but the way Richard expresses his artistic side and shows the affection he feels for people by the care with which he prepares and serves the food.

Richard and the Olive Garden
By Robert Bringardner

Those of us who know Richard are well aware of the fact that Richard is something of a "foodie" or "aficionado of food and drink." During his annual December visits to Florida to visit his mother-in-law, we would always seek out the top restaurants in the Daytona Beach area and hope that it met his demanding standards. One time, I believe it was in the early 1990's, my mother and I had discovered a new Italian restaurant in Daytona Beach. It was called simply "The Olive Garden." We felt certain that Richard would be thrilled with this new dining opportunity! Unfortunately, the restaurant was not acceptable for such a "foodie." The wine and food quality were both below par and the service personnel were apparently neither willing nor empowered to solve problems that occurred. As we departed, a hapless employee said something like "I hope that we do better next time!" That's when Richard uttered those immortal words: "There won't be a next time!"

His words are remembered and repeated to this day. I can't count the times that my mother has used them to define an experience that will NOT be repeated. And to the best of my knowledge, Richard has never seen the inside of an Olive Garden since that day.

Math Sightings in Europe
By Barbara Bringardner Geller

As many of you know, Richard and I love to go to Europe for our summer vacation. We have travelled in France as well as many other countries. We love the fine dining (no surprise here) and also biking through the charming historic countryside. But, what many of you did not know is that many of our vacations have included some very cool math sightings. I would like to tell you about a few of them now.

First, there was the art gallery at the Pompidou Center in Paris where we came across a room lit up with numbers of the Fibonacci Sequence mounted on the walls in blue neon!

Then another time, when we were walking along the shore of Lake Geneva, after a very large and impressive meal at Girardet Restaurant, we came across a stone statue of the letter pi, with the digits of pi carved into it out to hundreds of decimal places.

Photograph by Barbara Geller

And then there was the very cool bar and restaurant in the small working class town of Crewe in Northern England. The name of the establishment was Pi r squared. The bar area was of course in the shape of a circle and rotated 360 degrees.

And then once in Cannes, France, we passed by a hotel named the pi hotel with a very cool Ferrari parked outside. I am not sure which

Richard was more impressed with, the name of the hotel or the Ferrari. Actually, I think the Ferrari!

Photograph by Barbara Geller

But the coolest sighting of all was of Mr. Richard Geller, a New York City math teacher, sitting at a café in a very stylish area of the French Riviera, proof reading math team competitions while his wife Barbara enjoyed the local ambience and indulged in a little Campari cocktail.

Crossing the Delaware River
By Dick Shulman and Carol Sterling

One day while we were visiting Barbara and Richard in Bucks County, we went out for a stroll along the Delaware River. At one point, while we were crossing one of the bridges, out of nowhere we hear someone shout "Mr. Geller!" Wouldn't you know, it turned out to be a former student of Richard's from Stuyvesant High School. He was eager to greet Richard and they enjoyed a pleasant chat. Apparently, this fellow had graduated from Stuyvesant many years earlier. Nonetheless, even after the passing of so many years, Richard had made a large impression on him. It must be wonderful to have that kind of impact on so many young people.

It is not possible to describe in a single anecdote Richard's warm kindness and considerateness, which we have always felt in our interactions with him. Likewise it is not possible to describe the obvious caring devotion between Barbara and Richard, and the way that it extends itself to encompass their friends.

Photograph by Barbara Geller

Eat, Drink and Be Merry
By Roberta Kiver and Dick Roth

Eat

Ah yes Richard is the consummate chef! For our engagement announcement celebration in Cape May, Richard brought a lemon tart. He had just finished a day at cooking classes and voila there was the Lemon Tart for all of us to enjoy.

Drink

Then there was our wedding celebration, with raspberry rasmopolitans. We think Richard will remember it, but then those rasmopolitans were really good!

Be Merry

Richard and Barbara have been gracious hosts to us both in the city and at their Bucks County home. Food, of course, is part of these merry memories. Too many good meals to recount, but it was in Bucks County that Richard introduced us to his fabulous fried skate. So tender, so delicious, who would have known! It was also at Bucks County that we enjoyed a weekend of picture puzzle piecing together. Richard and his assistants considered it a challenge and the puzzle was completed overnight.

The Five Forks Meal
By Sandi Levy and Sol Adwar

Aside from sharing many of life's milestones with Barbara and Richard, such as visits to Miami and New York, divorces, weddings, bar mitzvahs, and birthdays, the one event that really stands out from all the rest was that day Barbara and Richard invited us to their weekend home in Bucks County, Pennsylvania. It was a Friday afternoon. After they both had worked hard all day, they picked us up in the city, and drove us in, slow, turtle-paced traffic to their house in Pennsylvania. Upon arrival, a few hours later, Barbara invited us to a glorious hot-tub bubble bath in the upstairs bathroom. Due to Sol's generous weight, much water was displaced and there were bubbles everywhere! After cleaning up the suds we went downstairs, drank some delicious wine and sat down to enjoy a feast which Richard had created while we were bathing and cleaning.

Showtime! The table had been set beautifully, yet strangely. There were five, yes five forks at each setting! I had never seen so many forks. I thought it was the wine! But no, it was intentional. Barbara and Richard explained that we would be having a five-entrée dinner. My Lord! Who knew! One fork for each entrée! It was a good thing there were only four of us! We remember the special salad. There were lots of greens, berries, nuts, goat cheese, and raspberry dressing. Delicious! There was also warm nut bread from a very special bakery in New York (Bouley, we think). Then there was a cat fish appetizer. We couldn't figure out when they had the time to marinate it. It was all the best! Of course throughout dinner, the wine glasses were never empty. We're so sorry, we don't remember what came next. Perhaps it was the wine. All we know is that it was the best five-course dinner we ever had!

In Search of a Vega Gourmet
By Harold A. Geller

I must admit that I have found it somewhat humorous, all these stories about Richard and gourmet food. You see, I can remember when Richard ate food that no one, except maybe Vega Texans, would call gourmet food. I believe it was 2003, and I had decided to drive to California in August to see a few friends and our long lost brother Allan. When I mentioned this to Richard, he thought he might tag along with me at least for the outgoing trip. So Richard joined me on the road to California. Driving in the Geller fashion, we left Virginia on I think it was a Tuesday morning, and drove through the day and night. Finally, late Wednesday afternoon we decided to stop in the vicinity of Amarillo, Texas. However, I thought it might be better to avoid the morning rush hour of Amarillo, so I thought we should drive on to Vega, Texas, about 25 miles west of Amarillo. We got to Vega, Texas about five in the afternoon. We first got a room at the best hotel in Vega, which isn't saying much. I think it was a Comfort Inn. Anyhow, there wasn't any restaurant near the hotel so we set out to find a restaurant within which to eat. We drove by a couple of small Mexican restaurants, but they didn't look too appealing, and Richard was concerned about my being a vegetarian and them having anything I might eat. Well, after driving through the entire town of Vega, we ended up settling on an eatery near the highway. I don't recall what Richard got, but I ordered a bunch of side orders of vegetables. We were even able to see the cook prepare the food. For my vegetables, she took out canned vegetables and opened the can, and used the microwave to heat up the vegetables. After our gourmet meal <chuckle>, Richard and I went to the Dairy Queen for dessert. Who could beat that for a gourmet meal with Richard!

By the way, on that trip out to California, we did stop at the Grand Canyon, for Richard's first and only look at it. We also visited with Lisa, and managed to see Jason as well, in Las Vegas. In San Francisco, we joined up with Barbara, who flew back to New York City with Richard, as I continued my journey to visit my friends Mitch and Janice Hobish in Manhattan. Manhattan, Montana that is.

Richard Geller's 65th Birthday Song
Lyrics written and performed by
Ronnie Jayne
"A Song For You Productions"

(Sing to "Oh, Carol")

Oh Richard – Many things you like
From gourmet cooking – To riding your bike
You're famous – When your class is done
'Cause you start yelling – "Math is # 1"

But you're only kidding – You know better
As you have confessed
Really it's family – And you have the best
You're devoted to your dear wife, Barbara
Lisa, Jason too
Oh Richard – You know they all love you.

(Sing to "When I'm 64")

Richie you're raised in Brooklyn, New York
By your Mom and Dad
Brother Allan and the youngest, Harold, too
As the first, they looked up to you.
From Brooklyn College – to Chapel Hill
Then back home you arrived
Masters in teaching – and now you're reaching – Almost 65.

You're teaching math at Stuyvesant High
Former Math Team Coach
GRF Test Preparation's what you do
Barry and Ken are partners with you
Whether in class or doing test prep
For excellence, you strive
Teaching tough classes – Not for the masses – Turning 65

(Bridge)
Met your wife at Marymount
Where Barbara made her questions count
In Switzerland you made a plan
Propose in Crissier
Years later – you've kept the bill
And bottle – from – Girardet

In Ken and Barry – you've got great friends
For so many years
Whether it's a Rao's for a monthly meal
Or Ranger games – You root with such zeal
They knew you in you – taxi cab days
Weekends you would drive
Those years are by – no "taxi high" – You're – Turning 65

You're so respected – Winning awards
So active are you
There you go a-wheeling in your bicycle pants
Sometimes New York, sometimes in France
Sharing your knowledge, sharing a meal
Your strong bonds have thrived
You've always proved that – You can still move, at – Almost 65

Everyone's cheering – Now that you're nearing
The Age of 65.

The Last Days of Life

Monday August 22, 2011

Richard had thoracentesis performed at
    NYU Medical Center
    32nd and 1st Ave
    2nd floor interventional radiology

Richard has having trouble breathing, was feeling very uncomfortable, and was very bloated in his stomach. On the prior Wednesday, Dr Pavlick had confirmed fluid in Richard's right side by physical examination and a chest x-ray. She suggested that Richard could wait for the BRAF/MEK inhibitor which was going to be first given on 8/24 to take effect or, if he was too uncomfortable, could have the fluid drained. Over the weekend Richard became very uncomfortable and early Monday morning we drove to Dr Pavlick's office where Richard saw the nurse practitioner Rashne (sp?). She wrote up a prescription and sent us the NYU Medical Center on 1st Ave for the procedure.

Dr Charles performed the procedure, taking before and after chest x-rays. 3.5 liters of fluid were drained. Richard was on the table for about 4 hours while it drained. Dr Charles looked at the chest x-ray done after the procedure and told Richard that everything was fine.

Wednesday August 24, 2011

Richard met with Dr Anna Pavlick NYU
Dr Anna Pavlick, Principal Investigator
Claire Stein, clinical research nurse

Statistics:
Weight: 148.6 w/shoes
Temperature: 98.5
Blood pressure: 118/83
Heart Rate: 90
Oxygen: 93
Waist measurement at belly button: 35"

General
Dr Pavlick explained that Richard's cancer had probably developed resistance to the BRAF inhibitor in both the pleural cavity and in the

abdomen. She said there are 3 alternate pathways that the cancer typically finds to get around the BRAF inhibitor and these pathways all meet downstream at MEK. Dr Pavlick added that the cancer in Richard's lungs and in his bone still seems stable indicating that the cancer in these organs is still being blocked by the BRAF inhibitor. This is why the combination of BRAF/MEK inhibitors is effective in patients like Richard. It blocks the cancer at both points in the pathway.

Physical
Dr Pavlick explained that the 3.5 liters of fluid that was drained from Richard's right pleural cavity on Monday was fluid that was secreted by the new cancer in Richards's pleural lining. After examining Richard, she said the cancer in Richard's abdomen is probably also secreting fluid. She said she could feel some but it probably was not enough to require being drained. She said she expected that the new drug would take care of this. She added that Richard's liver doesn't seem enlarged so the cancer is probably stable there too.

She said the discomfort in Richard's abdomen and his nausea was probably caused by the small tumors in Richard's abdomen irritating the general area. Again, this should improve in a few days after Richard starts to take this drug.

Combo BRAF/MEK trial
Richard's new drug regiment will be as follows:
For the first 14 days of each 28 day cycle
- Each morning: BRAF Inhibitor (RO5185426) 720 mg

  MEK Inhibitor (GDC – 0973/XL518) 60mg
- Each evening: BRAF Inhibitor (RO5185426) 720 mg

For the second 14 days of each 28 day cycle
- Each morning: BRAF Inhibitor (RO5185426) 720 mg

- Each evening: BRAF Inhibitor (RO5185426) 720 mg

Dr Pavlick said Richard should see results with his next visit, one week from today. She said the other patient on this combo trial at NYU had cysts under his skin that shrunk significantly so that they were too small to biopsy after only 2 weeks of treatment. She was expecting comparable results for Richard.

As part of the study, Richard had to reduce his dose of the BRAF inhibitor from 960 mg 2 times a day down to 720 mg 2 times a day for one week. The 720 mg dosage is what is required for this new BRAF/MEK combo trial. Also, as part of the study, several blood samples were taken from Richard at intervals the day before the MEK inhibitor was added and at similar intervals on the day Richard started taking the MEK inhibitor.

Wednesday August 31, 2011

Richard met with Dr Anna Pavlick NYU
Richard and Barbara were present
Dr Anna Pavlick, Principal Investigator
Claire Stein, clinical research nurse

Statistics:
Weight: 152.3 w/shoes
Temperature: 97.4
Blood pressure: 123/80
Heart Rate: 72
Oxygen: 96

Physical
Dr Pavlick examined Richard. She said his belly seemed softer today as opposed to last week. She said in general the tumors get softer and then liquefy and go away as they recede. She said this was an indication that the new treatment is beginning to work. She also listened to Richard's lungs and said that his lungs were much better. She said last time the liquid was high in his right lung (3/4 of the way up) but now is much lower (1/4 of the way up). She added that the left side is clear. Lastly, she checked the growth on the back of Richard's left leg and said it was a pimple probably caused by ingrown hair. This is a typical side effect found with the combo trial. She said Richard should put a hot compress on it to bring it out and then a band aid with bacitracin.

Pleural Fluid Testing
Regarding testing of the pleural fluid that was drained from Richard's right cavity on 8/22/11, Dr Pavlick said it was not tested. She said if they did test it, they would say it was cancer. When I asked about testing for mutations and other information about how Richard's cancer had progressed around the BRAF block, she said that NYU pathology was not equipped to test these specifics of Richard's DNA and even if

they were, it would not be helpful now. She said 99% of the patients end up developing a pathway through to MEK and the drug Richard is taking is intended for this.

Changing the Cohort for the BRAF/MEK combo trial
Both Claire and Dr Pavlick independently stated that Richard could not move to another cohort or increase his dose of the BRAF or MEK inhibitors or change the frequency of dosage. Dr Pavlick added that the MEK inhibitor has a long half-life and that is why there is a 14 days on and then a 14 days off protocol. She added that the higher doses resulted in greater toxicity which has been a problem.

PD-1 trial at Sloan Kettering
I asked Dr Pavlick if she ever heard back from Sloan Kettering about this trial. She said the trial has been closed because of bad toxicity experienced at John Hopkins. She said the drug manufacturer was looking at ways to better address the toxicity.

Amendment D for the protocol Richard is on.
Claire said that she recently received protocol changes (amendment D) from the drug manufacturer. She said there were very few changes to Richard's protocol but that they mainly involved the timing of the ECG and blood tests Richard is involved with. She said the next cohort is starting soon and they are completing the paperwork and getting people signed up for it. She said she would tell us more as she knows more.

LDH Level
Claire said Richard's LDH level has been decreasing since a peak of 857 on 8/9. (8/9: 857, 8/17/11: 814, 8/24/11: 747) They were not able to give me the LDH level yet for today. Claire said for melanoma, this is not a clear indicator of cancer growth but it can represent disease.

Next steps:
Friday 9/2/11 at 7:30am: The trial requires Richard to complete a PET scan which shows the metabolic uptake for tumor growth. Claire said this is required for the study and will not be used to evaluate Richard's disease progression. She said there are no CT images ordered with this test. These scans would normally be used to determine tumor size. Richard can take his morning medication before arriving for the test.
Tues 9/6/11: Richard should go to the 5th floor where he will be all day and where blood will be taken every 2 hours to evaluate specifics on how the drug is being processed by Richard.

Friday September 2, 2011

Beginning the night before and through the night, Richard was having trouble sleeping and breathing. On the prior Wednesday, after a physical exam, Dr Pavlick said the fluid was only ¼ of the way up Richard's lung. After Richard's PET scan the next Friday morning, Richard was feeling badly so we walked from the MedScan office on 40th and 2nd to Dr Pavlick's office at the NYU Cancer Center at 34th and 3rd. Richard was examined by Dr Ott, an associate of Dr Pavlick; by Crystal, a study nurse; and was seen by Kathy, the nurse practitioner. On examination, Crystal said it seemed the fluid in Richard's right lung was 2/3rds of the way up. Kathy FAXed a prescription to NYU Medical Canter for Richard to have the fluid drained and we walked over there.

Dr Sean Farquharson with the help of an MD 'fellow' Cathy, performed the procedure. When I told Dr Farquharson that 3.5 liters of fluid was drained about 1 ½ weeks ago on 8/22, he said he wanted to biopsy the fluid this time.

In total, 2 liters of fluid were drained with the first fluid being reserved for a biopsy. Richard was on the table for about 4 hours while it drained. After the procedure, a new chest x-Ray was performed. Dr Farquharson came out to explain the results saying that there was still a lot of fluid in Richard's lungs. Based on a chest x-ray Richard had before the 8/22 procedure, Dr Farquharson said the fluid was now approximately at the same level that it was before the 3.5 liters were drained on 8/22. I said and Dr Farquharson confirmed that this meant approximately 5.5 liters of fluid had collected since 8/22. Dr Farquharson tried to reach Dr Pavlick to discuss next steps but left a message instead saying it was not an emergency and he would talk with Dr Pavlick on Tuesday and get back to us. He said Richard should probably stay over night in the hospital to allow the remaining fluid to drain. He added that it was not safe to force the fluid to drain too quickly. He said Richard could get a PleurX® which is a tube that would allow Richard to drain the fluid himself everyday or get a pleurdesis procedure performed which closes the gap where fluid currently collects between the pleura and the lung (I think I got this right). The nurse in interventional radiology later added that if Richard was experiencing any problem, he could always go to the emergency room and the attending physician would be contacted.

Next steps:
Richard will wait to hear from Dr Pavlick or Dr Farquharson on Tuesday about the appropriate next steps to address the current and future fluid accumulations.

Wednesday, September 7, 2011

Richard met with Rashne (nurse practitioner) and Claire (study nurse) at NYU.

Note: Richard was scheduled to see Dr Pavlick but she was late driving in from NJ because of traffic, accidents, and road closures. We actually saw her as we were leaving the building and she asked about Richard's breathing.

Statistics:
Weight: 149.9 w/shoes
Temperature: 97.4
Blood pressure: 127/79
Heart Rate: 67
Oxygen: 97

Response to Questions:
Flu Shot: Rashne said they recommended that Richard get a flu shot. She said they recommend a flu shot for all patients except those on the IPI drug (Yervoy) since it is a form of immunotherapy. The flu shot introduces small amounts of the flu virus into the body to stimulate the immune system which could interfere with the IPI drug. She said they expected to get the flu vaccine on September 6 so they should have it soon. Richard could get the flu shot from Dr Pavlick's office. Richard said he wanted to wait for 2 weeks anyway.

Pleural Effusion: Rashne said Richard's pleural effusion was probably a result of fluid that was released by inflammation or it could be malignant cells. She said it was a byproduct of the cancer and there were not any cancer tumors in the pleural space itself. She added that it was not an infection and said it was more likely to be an exudate and not a transudate effusion since transudate indicates an infection. When I asked about the biopsy that was requested by Dr Sean Farquharson, the NYU doctor who performed the thoracentesis procedure on 9/2, Rashne said NYU cytology would complete the fluid analysis and results should be available in about 7 days. She added that it was likely that the fluid was loculated which means it possibly got into pockets which could not be drained so easily.

Rashne said they anticipated that Richard's treatment would address the pleural effusion problem and they are hoping it will dissipate on its own. She added that the other NYU patient who is on Richard's drug had to wait one month before he experienced a sustained response to the drug. When I asked if this patient was on the 14 days on and 14 days off protocol that Richard is on, she said yes. She said sometimes drugs that take a longer time to work will also have a more sustained response (i.e. longer duration of response). She added, however, that if Richard's breathing becomes worst, he should have the fluid drained again. If this does happen, they would consider giving him a pleural catheter so he could drain the fluid himself at home.

9/2/11 Pet Scan: Rashne said she did not know the results of the PET scan Richard had on Friday. She said we could discuss it next Wednesday. She said it was not critical now to review the results since they would not influence Richard's treatment plan. She said the test was something required by the FDA to show if there is any activity now. She added that since it was only a PET Scan and not a CT Scan also, it would not measure the tumors corresponding to the metabolic activity and there could be many sources of metabolic activity other than cancer tumors (e.g., healing tissue from a bruise, healing from Friday's Thoracentesis procedure, etc).

Pain in left side of neck: Rashne said this was probably muscular pain maybe related to the way Richard is sleeping. She said patients sometimes develop referred pain. For example, cancer in the liver can result in a pain in the right shoulder. Also, sometimes patients feel pain in a healthy liver because the cancer drugs are being broken down by the liver. Normally, she cannot feel a patient's liver which is below the right case unless the liver is enflamed.

Physical:
Rashne listened to Richard's breathing and said the left lung was fine but she could hear that there was still fluid in the right lung. After reading the 8/8/11 PET/CT Scan, she said the liver seemed to be a little bit improved from the 6/11 CT Scan and was continuing to respond to the BRAF inhibitor. She added that the cancer in Richard's abdominal cavity was actually in the fatty covering over the omentum (I think I got this right) and also in the back of the abdominal cavity.

Next Steps:
If Richard's breathing becomes more difficult, he should come into the office (or go to the NYU emergency room if it is a weekend) and ask to have the fluid drained again. Dr Pavlick, Richard attending physician, will always be contacted.

Monday September 12, 2011

Over the weekend, Richard was having trouble breathing and felt short of breath, particularly when exerting himself in any way. This morning, we went to see the staff at NYU Cancer Center. They arranged for Richard to get fluid drained from his right pleural space using a thoracentesis procedure. After about 4 1/2 hours, they drained 3.3 liters. The attending physician, Dr Kovacs, did a sonogram after the procedure and reported that all of the accumulated fluid had been drained. This is important because the last time Richard completed this procedure on 9/2/11, they drained 2 liters but said there was still a significant amount of fluid remaining. Also, no suction was used to drain the fluid. The other 3 times fluid was drained, some suction was applied to remove the fluid.

Dr Kovacs also explained that Richard may be accumulating pleural fluid because the cancer in Richard's lymph nodes may be blocking the fluid from draining from the pleural space.

Richard was very tired after the procedure but reported that he was breathing much better. Also, when eating salad at dinner, Richard started heaving and threw up clear vomit. On the next Wednesday, Rashne said the procedure probably irritated Richard's lungs and the clear throw-up was probably mucus from the lungs.

Dr Pavlick thinks this general problem will resolve itself as soon as the trial drug Richard is taking responds better. Dr Pavlick already thinks the drug is reducing the cancer in Richard's abdomen. We hope to get the same results in Richard's in lungs.

The male nurse in the recovery area explained that Richard could come into the emergency room over the weekend to have this procedure performed. If he did, they would call in the attending physician in the unit who was on call that weekend. The attending physicians in the area are: Dr Charles, Dr Farquharson, Dr Kovacs, and Dr Gross, who Richard has not had yet. The nurse added that Dr Charles lives very close. The nurse said that Dr Charles seems to him to be the most competent.

Wednesday September 14, 2011

Richard met with Rashne (nurse practitioner) and Claire (study nurse) at NYU.
Dr Pavlick was out-of-town at a leadership class.

Statistics:
Weight: 144.7 w/shoes
Temperature: 98.6
Blood pressure: 127/79
Heart Rate: 84
Oxygen: 97
Glucose: 95
LDH: 694 non specific

Response to Questions:
Fluid Effusion
Rashne said she reviewed the 9/2 cytology report from the fluid Richard had drained on 9/2 and said there was no malignancy in the fluid. Instead, she said it was a reactive fluid which was probably caused by the tumors in Richard's lungs and abdomen. She said tumors in both areas could result in drainage in Richard's pleural space. She said, in general, the cancer causes irritation and secretes fluid which results in fluid accumulation. She added that there is no new cancer in Richard's lungs from the 9/2 PET Scan.

When Rashne examined Richard, she said there was still some small amount of fluid in Richard's right lung. She added, it seems the pockets were probably deloculated, allowing the fluid to be drained. She said the drug may have allowed the pockets to deloculate.

Rashne said that Dr Pavlick wanted Richard to wait for a full cycle for 4 weeks on the new drug before he has a catheter put in so he can drain the fluid himself or gets a pleurodesis procedure which closes the pleural space so fluid cannot accumulate. Richard is currently completing week 3 on the drug.

Other symptoms
Nausea: Richard reported some nausea the last 1 ½ weeks. Rashne said it was probably caused by the MEK drug even though Richard was

on an 'off period' for the drug and had not taken it for 1 week. Richard said he did not want to take any medicine for this. (Rashne said Compazine may have been previously recommended in Richmond for this.) Claire said that Richard should ask her before taking any drug to make sure it is cleared by the study.

Pain in left side of neck: Richard said he was still experiencing this pain. Rashne said she still thought this was muscular pain related to the way Richard is sleeping. She asked Richard if he had used a tennis ball on the back to loosen the muscle.

Heaving and clear vomit after 9/12/11 thoracentesis: Rashne said the procedure probably irritated Richard's lungs and the clear throw-up was probably mucus from the lungs.

Little bumps on back, abdomen, etc: I think Rashne said Richard should ask the dermatologist to look at this next Wednesday.

Physical and blood work:
Rashne said Richard's abdomen felt softer which means the drug is working. She also listened to Richard's heart and lungs and said everything seemed fine. On tapping Richard's right back, she said she could still hear some fluid in Richard's right lung.

Rashne and Claire both said that Richard's blood work looked good. When I asked about the **glucose** level, Rashne said it was 95 which is normal. When I asked about the **LDH**, she said it was 694 which is very good. (The normal range is 313-618.) I added that it has come down gradually from 8/9 when Richard had the CT/PET scan showing that the cancer had spread to the abdomen. The LDH was 857 then. Rashne added that the LDH level is a non specific indicator. She said generally that low numbers indicated a good prognosis. High numbers can indicate inflammation and are a tumor marker. Also, as tumors are treated and breakdown, the number can rise.

Diet
Rashne said the important thing for Richard is that he eat a balanced diet. She said for some cancers, there is a relationship between glucose level and cancer growth but this had not been shown for melanoma. She added that it was not important to eat a lot of protein either. She said a very high protein diet could be hard on the liver and pancreas. She said if Richard was interested, he could see the nutritionist, Linda C[?], who would recommend a balanced diet and would explain what

was meant by that. She also said that if Richard is having problems with loss of appetite, he should have small, frequent meals to maintain his weight.

Next Steps:
Next Wednesday will mark the end of cycle one. Richard will see the dermatologist, Dr Stein, at 9am in 7R in the hospital building. He will then see Dr Pavlick and Claire on the 9th floor. He will take his Wednesday am pills during the appointment, return left over pills from the first cycle and get new pills for the new cycle. He will also turn in his diary.

Richard's next CT/PET Scan is scheduled for 3 weeks from today, after week 6.

Monday September 19, 2011

Over the weekend, Richard was starting to have trouble breathing and was feeling very uncomfortable. By Monday morning, he said he was feeling the most uncomfortable ever. We went to Dr Pavlick's office early Monday and saw Claire, the study nurse, and Kathy Madden, the nurse practitioner. Kathy listened to Richard's symptoms (loss of appetite, some nausea, dry heaving in the evening, coughing, shortness of breath) and examined him. When she tapped Richard's back, she said his lungs were 'pretty full up'. She added that the nausea and loss of appetite symptoms may be a result of pressure from the pleural space but just in case, she said would move Richard's next CT scan up one week. Richard's next scan was originally scheduled for Friday, September 30.

At NYU hospital, Richard and I talked with Dr Charles. He looked at Richard's x-ray and said the pleural effusion was only on the right side, and not on the left side. When I told Dr Charles that Dr Pavlick's nurse practitioner reported that the fluid from Richard's 9/2/11 thorencentsis was not malignant but was reactive fluid, he added that the build-up of pleural fluid could have many different causes but it was not necessarily the result of active growing cancer in Richard's lungs. He said it could be irritation of the lungs. I asked about Richard's oxygen level which was 97. Dr Charles said that anything over 87 was ok. He said Richard's level is as high as it is because Richard has a good heart which compensates. Then I asked if the fluid was putting pressure on Richard's abdomen, he said he would include the abdominal area in the sonogram to find out. Later, he told Richard that there was very little fluid build-up in Richard's abdomen. Dr Charles explained the risks of a PleurX® catheter as: risk of infection and possible leak around the exit site. He said if we notice a problem, we should call their contact number. He said the PleurX® was semi-permanent and would last for many months. He said they would inset it in Richard's back. He said it was flexible so Richard could sleep on it. Also, Richard can shower with it.

Dr Gross, a colleague of Dr Charles, performed the procedure. He drained 2 liters of fluid. Afterwards, the nurse gave us supplies that the visiting nurse who is coming tomorrow can use when she shows me how to drain the fluid. Also, after the procedure, I asked about Richard using an incentive spirometer to strengthen and expand his lungs. Kathy, Dr Pavlick's nurse practitioner, said this was a good idea and arranged for Richard to get one.

Wednesday September 21, 2011

Richard met with Dr Pavlick, Rajni Kannan (nurse practitioner) and Crystal (study nurse) at NYU. Claire was with another patient on the 5th floor.

Statistics:
Weight: 147.4 w/shoes
Temperature: 98.3
Blood pressure: 127/79
Heart Rate: 94
Oxygen: ?
Glucose: ?
Sodium: very low – eat salty foods and drink Gatorade
LDH: 753 up slightly because of Richard's PleurX® procedure which caused inflammation

Response to Questions:
Fluid Effusion: Rajni gave me a copy of the cytology report from 9/2/11 which analyzed the right pleural fluid. The report said Richard's right pleural fluid was: "Negative for malignant cells. Chronic Inflammation. Reactive Mesothelial Cells." Dr Pavlick later stated that Richard's enlarged and bumpy liver was possibly irritating his diaphragm each time he takes a breath. This could be the cause of the large volume of pleural fluid.

Rajni said the visiting nurse will come to teach me how to drain the pleural fluid. She added that I only need to change the bandages once a week. She also said I should limit the amount drained to 750ml/day because of Richard electrolyte imbalance (see below under low sodium.) She added that when I only get out 500ml, I can drain every other day instead of every day.

Barbara added that the attending physician who completed Richard's PleurX® procedure on 9/19/11 (Dr Gross) said that a sonogram at that time of Richard's chest and abdomen showed that he did not have much fluid in his abdominal cavity.

Coughing: Dr Pavlick said the coughing is probably caused by the irritation to Richard's pleural lining.

Fatigue: Dr Pavlick said Richard's fatigue is probably a result of the disease, his trouble breathing, and the treatment.

Nausea: May be caused by the drug. Rajni suggested taking prochlorperazine for mild nausea and reserving ondansetron for severe nausea since if can cause constipation and headaches.

Loss of Appetite: Dr Pavlick said this was probably caused by the disease.

Heaving without throwing up: This is probably a result of increased acid reflex caused by pressure on the belly. Rajni suggested taking nexium once a day. We worked out a schedule where Richard would take it each morning, ½ hour before taking his medicine. For example, take the nexium at 6 am, his experimental drug at 6:30 am and then have breakfast at 7:30 am. (As of 9/24, Richard has not taken Nexium again.) A few minutes later, when Richard took his medicine in the doctor's office, he started heaving. Crystal said Richard took the medicine with water too quickly. She said he should take it more slowly, with smaller sips of water, and without gulping it.

Low Sodium: Dr Pavlick and Rajni said Richard's sodium is very low. They suggested he eat salty French fries, Campbells chicken soup, or potato chips. They also said he had an electrolyte imbalance and should drink Gatorade. (As of 9/24, Richard has done a very good job of following this advice.) Rajni added that I should limit the amount of fluid taken from Richard's lungs to 750ml/day which we have done.

Flu Shot: Dr Pavlick said a flu shot would not exclude Richard from any treatment but it might delay treatment. She suggested that Richard wait to get a flu shot until after he knows what his next treatment will be. She added that it was still early to get a flu shot. As a practice Rajni said they had not decided whether to recommend that their patients on IPI take a flu shot.

Next CT Scan: Dr Pavlick said we should keep to the original schedule for Richard's CT scan (Friday, 9/30). She said Richard is starting up again on the MEK drug and we should get the benefit of the drug before the scan.

Next Treatment: Caroline (Richard's BRAF study nurse) said that Dr Pavlick has a number of new trials opening up. She added that Dr Pavlick has been looking for some good studies to make available to her patients. One is an monoclonal antibody drug which is a type of immunotherapy. She said that NYU would not be getting the PD-1 trial.

Physical and blood work: Dr Pavlick listened to Richard's lungs, heart and abdomen. She said his right lung seemed to be about ½ full.

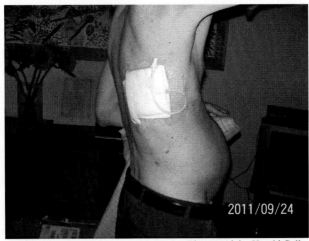

Photograph by Harold Geller

> Wednesday September 28, 2011

Richard met with Dr Pavlick and Claire (study nurse) at NYU.

Statistics:
Weight: 148.0 w/shoes
Temperature: 97.6
Blood pressure: 108/77
Heart Rate: 73
Oxygen: 96
Sodium: still low 131– eat salty foods and drink Gatorade
LDH: 741 down slightly from last week

Response to Questions:
Symptoms: Fluid Effusion: I told Rajni that I have been draining 750 ml/day using Richard's PleurX® catheter since 9/22 when I was trained to drain the fluid. Rajni said I should continue to drain 750 ml/day since Richard's sodium level is still low (i.e., 131). When Dr Pavlick examined Richard, she said his right lung was ¾ aerated which is better than last week.

Symptoms: Abdominal Cramping: Richard reported that he occasionally has abdominal cramps. Dr Pavlick gave him a prescription for a drug (se-donna pb hyos elixir) that he can take as required. It is used for babies for colic. It is a liquid that does not need to be digested. You take one teaspoon as needed. It works in 10 minutes.

Symptoms: Skin Rash: Dr Pavlick noted that Richard has a heavier rash on his back than before. Richard said this does not bother him.

Other symptoms: Dr Pavlick encouraged Richard to take medication for cramps, nausea, and acid reflux, as required. When Richard said again that he does not like to take drugs, Dr Pavlick asked me to encourage him to do this.

Examination
Dr Pavlick examined Richard and said she thinks he might be doing a little better since he started on the MEK inhibitor again last Wednesday, 9/21. She added that his belly seems a little less distended and the left lobe of Richard's liver is not worse. As part of the protocol he will continue on the MEK inhibitor until next Wednesday, October 5. (The protocol is 2 weeks on the MEK inhibitor followed by 2 weeks

off. He takes the BRAF inhibitor every day.) She added that the MEK drug may be responsible for any improvement in the last week.

(My impression is that Richard got a little worse when he was off of the MEK drug and then maybe got a little better after he got back on it again. It is not clear and certainly very subtle.)

Dr Pavlick asked questions about how much Richard is teaching (5 classes every day) and noted that his white blood platelets are good and other blood counts are good.

CT/PET Scan
Subsequent to the appointment, Richard had the scans on Friday, 9/30. We will discuss results with Dr Pavlick on Wednesday, 10/5.

BRAF/MEK Combo Trial:
I asked Claire if the trial is set up to allow patients to move to a higher dose if their disease progresses on a lower dose. (Richard takes 720mg of BRAF twice a day every day and 60 mg of MEK once a day on a two weeks on, two weeks off schedule.) I mentioned that trials of anit-PD-1 are set up this way. Claire responded that this was not possible on the BRAF/MEK combo trial that Richard is on.

Saturday October 1, 2011

Notes by Barbara

MDX 1106 (anti-PD-1)

Johns Hopkins: I talked with the melanoma research nurse (Alice Pons) at Johns Hopkins. She said they have one spot open on the MDX 1106 (anti-PD-1) trial. She thinks this is a very good trial. It is a phase 1b trial. Patients are randomized to a dose level of .3, 1 or 10 mg/kg. If a patient has symptomatic progression after being on a lower dose, they can be moved up to a higher dose They are also planning to open a phase 1b trial of PD-L1 (MDX 1105) in late October or early November.

Sloan Kettering: The anti-PD-1 trial is closed at Sloan Kettering. The anti-PD-1 /IPI combo trial has a long wait list. According to Sarah's friend Ping's discussion with Dr Carvajal, additional PD-1 trials may be opening soon. According to Ruthie, the study nurse at Sloan Kettering, the anti-PD-1/IPI combo trial uses a dose of 3 mg/kg or

10mg/kg of IPI and .3 mg/kg, 1 mg/kg, 3 mg/kg, or 10 mg/kg of MDX 1106.

Dana Farber: The melanoma research nurse at Dana Faber (Megan) said the anti-PD-1 trial has 2 open spots. The dosing is .1, .3 or 1 mg/kg. Patients can be moved to a higher dose if their disease advances at a lower dose. They are also planning to open a trial of PD-L1 in the next month or so.

Yale Medical School: I understand Yale has a trial of both anti-PD-1 and anti-PD-1/IPI combo. I am still trying to get in touch with them.

Testing for B7-H1 surface expression
The July 1 2010 issue of *Journal of Clinical Oncology* reported a correlation between cell surface expression of B7-H1 to a PR (partial response) in the Phase 1 trial of anti-PD-1. I have asked the study nurses about being treated for this cell surface expression and was told it is not being done. Subsequently, Emma talked with the head of the immunohistochemistry lab at the University of Chicago who said they do not have the stain required. Emma expressed some concern that testing for B7-H1 surface expression may still be used in research only and a dependable protocol has not yet been developed. Emma plans to look into this in more detail.

Wednesday October 5, 2011

Richard met with Dr Pavlick, Caroline (study nurse), and Kathy (nurse practitioner) at NYU. Richard and Barbara were present.

Statistics:
Weight: 147.5 w/shoes
Temperature: 97.1
Blood pressure: 102/69
Heart Rate: 72
Oxygen: 96
Sodium: still low 129– eat salty foods like pickles, olives, cold cuts and drink Gatorade
LDH: 816 up from last week maybe because cancer cells are dying off

Results from 9/30 CT/PET Scan
Dr Pavlick said Richard had very good results from his CT/PET Scan. There is no new cancer. His lungs are stable as are the lymph nodes in his chest. Also, the abdomen is stable. Richard's liver is dramatically

better. There is no uptake in the liver legion. She said it is not active and would eventually reduce in size and, as a result, reduce the amount of the pleural fluid accumulated.

Results from 10/5 blood work
Caroline said Richard white blood counts, platelets and red blood cell counts are all very good. Dr Pavlick said Richard's sodium level is still low. She said his LDH is higher at 816 but it is a non-specific measure and as cell die it releases LDH as the cancer cells die. This could account for the LDH increase. She added that Richard's Creatine Kinase is very high at 416 (average is 30-170). She said is caused by the MEK drug and will go down when the amount of MEK in Richard's system is lower.

Symptoms: Pleural Effusion: CT scan said it was still moderate in size but better than the last CT Scan. I continue to drain 750 ml/day.

Symptoms: Abdominal Cramping: 4 times last night after yoghurt at 4pm. Took SE-DONNA PB HYOS ELIXIR and was drowsy and slept for 20 minutes. Then had diarrhea 3 times before dinner.

Symptoms: Diarrhea: Last night, Richard had diarrhea 3 times before dinner and then 3 more times thru the night and this morning. Dr Pavlick and Kathy suggested that Richard take 2 Imodium on onset and then 1 Imodium with every episode thereafter, up to a maximum 4-5 pills in a 24 hour period. If Richard's diarrhea becomes worst, he should give the office a call. They will prescribe limodal which is a stronger anti-diarrhea medicine.

Symptoms: Acid Reflex: Even though Richard is not having these symptoms now, Kathy said Richard should take pantoprazole 40mg (similar to the Nexium) every morning 30 minutes before Richard's morning medication. Kathy said it can take 5-7 days for the drug to work.

In general, Kathy said GI distress is a common side effect of the MEK drug. This should become less prevalent when Richard is in the 2 week 'off period' and is not taking MEK but only taking the BRAF drug.

Symptoms: Appetite Richard says his appetite is up and down. He said last night he was not interested in eating that much but forced himself to eat anyway.

Examination
Kathy examined Richard but made few comments.

Visiting Nurses
Dr Pavlick and Kathy said it is fine to stop the Visiting Nurse visits for now. If needed, we can start it up again.

Wednesday October 12, 2011

Richard met with Dr Pavlick, Claire (study nurse), Rajni (nurse practitioner), and Dr Pavlick at NYU. Richard and Barbara were present.

Statistics:
Weight: 152.6 w/shoes (up a little possibly due to pleural fluid)
Temperature: 98.2
Blood pressure: 107/70
Heart Rate: 84
Oxygen: 95
Sodium: 134 – almost within normal range
LDH: 823

Pleural Effusion
Beginning this past weekend, Richard has started to feel shortness of breath again. I drained .85 liter and 1 liter on Sunday Oct 10 and Monday Oct 11, respectively. (I have been draining .75 liter every day since I started on 9/22/11, except for last Saturday when I only drained .4 liter because of a problem with the PleurX® bottle.) Rajni and Dr Pavlick both said it was OK to drain 1 liter whenever Richard feels short of breath. Claire said the fluid is caused by irritation or by the tumors actually excreting the fluid. Dr Pavlick and Rajni added that patients on the MEK drug do seem to have more fluid accumulation. They both said that Richard had a lot of fluid accumulation.

Claire said it is not good to drain too much fluid at one time because the body tries to equalize the pressure and could pull fluid out of the vascular space which could cause a drop in blood pressure.

Results from 10/12 blood work
Dr Pavlick looked at Richard's blood work and said his protein and albumin levels were slightly up from last week which could mean that Richard's small intestine was able to absorb protein which is a good thing. Based on my questions, she also looked at Richard's neutrophil (81.1% with a normal range of 34.0-76.9%) and lymphocyte (7.3% with a normal range of 21.8 – 53.1%) levels which are both out of normal range. She added that neutrophil is used to fight bacterial infections and lymphocyte is used to fight viral infections. (I think I got this right.) She said these numbers could be a stress reaction due to the catheter.

Symptoms: Pain in neck: Rajni said this was probably not caused by the tumor at C1 since it seemed more like a muscular pain. She suggested that Richard use an Icy Hot Patch to relieve the pain.

Symptoms: Acid Reflex: Richard said he has begun to take pantoprazole 40mg (similar to the Nexium) every day. He did experience some heaving without throwing up during the past week (Mon night, Tues morning, and Wed morning only after taking water.)

Symptoms: Nausea: Richard said he experiences some nausea. Dr Pavlick said he could take the medicine they prescribed or drink ginger tea. She suggested he take it with his pills each day.

Symptoms: Appetite Richard says his appetite is up and down but generally less at night.

Symptoms: Fatigue Rajni said fatigue is unfortunately a side effect of every treatment they offer.

Examination
Rajni examined Richard and said she could hear gas in his abdomen. She noted that there was still rash on Richard's back.

Flu Shot
Rajni gave Richard a flu shot. Claire said this should not affect future treatments since only treatments that include IPI have a restriction on this and then only for 1 month. She added that the Morphotek trial at NYU (monoclonal antibodies) does not have a restriction due to this.

Wednesday October 19 and Thursday October 20, 2011

Richard met with Dr Pavlick, Crystal (study nurse)

Statistics:
Weight: 155.2 w/shoes (up due to accumulated fluid)
Temperature: 98.6
Blood pressure: 118/79
Heart Rate: 109
Oxygen: 93
Sodium: 128 – low because tumor cells are not allowing sodium to get into the small intestines
LDH: 1068 - higher because cancer has advanced

BRAF/MEK Combo trial
Dr Pavlick said based on Richard's blood test results, his symptoms, and how he looks; it seems that Richard's disease has progressed on the BRAF/MEK combo trial and he needs to move onto another treatment. She said the cancer in Richard's lungs and abdomen has progressed but the cancer in his liver and bones is stable. She said the tumors in Richard's lungs are mostly pleural based tumors around the outside of the right lung. After some discussion, she suggested Richard start with IPI in combination with BRAF. She said she has another patient who had the same treatment regiment as Richard (BRAF followed by BRAF/MEK). He has been on the BRAF/IPI combo for 3 weeks and has done very well. His LDH count dropped from 2000 to within normal range after 3 weeks on the treatment. In addition, he looks great and is back at work. She is hoping Richard will have the same experience. She said she is starting a third patient on this treatment this week.

IPI/BRAF Combo Trial
Richard started the first IPI infusion this morning (10/20/11). He will get additional infusions every 3 weeks. Some side effects that might develop are: diarrhea, skin rash either with or without itching, and possibly stomach cramps. We should call the doctor's office right away if anything develops so Richard can get treated for the side effect. She also said they will do lab checks for Richard's liver function since this can become a problem. Joanne, the oncology nurse, said that Linda, a nutritionist could help with diet. Also, a social worker and massage therapist is available. On Wednesday night, Barbara called Crystal to remind her that Richard had a flu shot one week ago. Crystal checked and found out that this would not be a problem since Richard had the

flu shot before starting the IPI treatment. In addition to the infusion for IPI, Dr Pavlick ordered an infusion of ½ liter of sodium. She said it would help some but Richard would not retain this in his blood because his protein level was low. Future IPI infusions are scheduled for November 10, December 1, and December 20. Richard will see Dr Ott for the first two visits and Dr Pavlick for the last one.

Crystal ordered the BRAF drug for Richard. He should get it Friday at the earliest. Medcom (Richard's prescription drug insurance) needs to work directly with Genentech to get the drug. They will call me when it is available. We should all Dr Pavlick as soon as we get it. Richard will take 960 mg twice a day. Kira Scripts called and the drug is now scheduled to arrive sometime on Monday.

Other treatments considered
IPI/Anti-PD1 combo: Dr Pavlick talked with Dr Carvajal about this trial. It is available at Sloan Kettering/Yale but has a waiting list of 20 patients and requires a 28 day 'wash out' period which Richard cannot tolerate. Dr Pavlick also commented that testing for the B7H1 expression on the tumor cell surface is only available in the research setting.
Anti-PD1: Barbara found out that 2 positions are still open for this study at Dana Farber but they require the 28 day 'wash out' period and would require that Richard relocate to Boston because of the protocol for required testing. Dr Pavlick said that someone at Johns Hopkins died when on the trial.

Adoptive Immunotherapy: Dr Pavlick said it takes 8 weeks for the cells to grow and there is only a 50-50 chance that they will grow successfully. She said she knew of 3 people on the trial and only 1 had their T cells grow after the 8 weeks. (Jean found another adoptive immunotherapy trial at NCI that requires less time to grow the T cells.)

CVT: Dr Pavlick said she talked with Dr Carvajal of Sloan Kettering on Wednesday night. He said the only trial Sloan Kettering can offer for Richard is CVT trial which is a type of chemotherapy with a 10-15% benefit rate. It is a type of chemotherapy with some amount of toxicity. It is a randomized trial of CVT vs CVT with a notch inhibitor. She did not recommend it.

Symptoms:
Difficulty Sleeping: Richard is having trouble sleeping at night because he cannot get comfortable in a reclined position. Richard is

not able to recline on his back or stomach and more recently not on either his left or right side. Dr Pavlick said she was surprised that the left side was a problem. After looking at Wednesday's CT/PET Scan, she said it might be because the cancer in the lymph node in the middle of the lung area compresses the area and make it difficult to breath. She suggested that a kind of targeted radiation called IMRT may be required. She added that IPI is a radiation sensitizer drug which could make the radiation more effective. This could make Richard symptomatically better. She also suggested that Richard have the fluid from his left pleural space drained. (Richard had .95 liters drained from the left pleural space on Thursday afternoon. This did not improve his ability to sleep or breath.)

Shortness of Breath and Difficulty Breathing: As of Sunday, 10/23/11 Richard feels shortness of breath with even the slightest exertion. Dr Pavlick said Richard was having trouble breathing because his lungs were compressed. She said oxygen was not helpful in this situation.

Fatigue: As of Sunday, Richard said he has no energy for anything.

Sweating: Dr Pavlick said this was tumor fever and was caused by the cancer.

Results from 10/19 blood work
Sodium: 128 and protein: 2.5 – low because tumor cells are not allowing sodium and protein to get into the small intestines
LDH: 1068 - higher because cancer has advanced

Friday October 21, 2011

Barbara Geller talked with Rajni

BRAF drug: This will be her next call. Genentech will send Richard a 15 day starter kit. We might get it on Monday or Tuesday or maybe on Saturday. (Dr Pavlick said we should call when we get it.) Kira Scripts called the house on Friday afternoon and said the drug will be arriving sometime on Monday.

Plan for breathing: Richard is not able to sleep at night because he cannot find a comfortable position. He ends up sleeping by sitting at the dining table with his head on a pillow on the table. Sometimes, he can sleep on his back in the recliner. He cannot sleep in the bed, even with the new wedge pillow. If Richard is still having trouble breathing at night on next visit (November 10) Dr Ott might order a IMRT which is targeted radiation on the area that is causing the problem. For now, we should keep the fluid drained. (Both Donna and the Dr Barry, the NYU doctor on call on Saturday, said that a pain reliever with a small amount of morphine may help since it would relax Richard a little bit and allow him to sleep. They both said the feeling one is trying to catch their breathe is not the same as not getting enough oxygen. Richard's oxygen level has consistently been in the low-mid nineties.)

Adema Fluid: This is building up because Richard's small intestines are not absorbing enough protein and salt to keep the fluid in his blood vessels. Gravity will cause the fluid to seep into the 3rd space in Richard's legs and feet. Raising the legs will only help temporarily because gravity will force the fluid down again. Debbie, the social worker, will arrange for a physical therapist to come to our apartment on Monday to help with a cane, walker or other strategies to make Richard more comfortable.

Left Pleural Space: I told Rajni that the doctor who performed the thoracentesis on Thursday afternoon drained 0.95 liters of fluid from Richard's left pleural space. Rajni said she talked with the doctor and he was hoping to delocuate an area in Richard's right pleural space with this procedure. (As of Saturday night, the fluid drained from Richard's right space seems to be decreasing, i.e., .240 liter Saturday night; so it is not clear that a new area in the right pleural space was deloculated.)

Sunday October 23, 2011

Hi All,

I finally wrote up my notes from Richard's appointments last week. They are attached.

Richard is still very fatigued and short of breath. We will probably go to the doctor's office tomorrow to see if anything can be done to improve his breathing.

Barbara

Tuesday October 25, 2011

I wanted to fill you in with what is happening with Richard. I know most of you already know these details.

Over the weekend, Richard's breathing got worse. It became labored with any exertion. Also, he could only sleep in an upright position with his head on a pillow on the dining room table. Any other position resulted in very labored breathing.

Yesterday, we went to NYU hospital, where they drained .8 liters of fluid from his left pleural space. He stayed overnight. Today, they plan to redo his right catheter to reach a fluid pocket that was missed by his current catheter.

This morning, Richard feels much better. His breathing is somewhat improved. As a matter of fact, he is sleeping well now in the hospital bed.

Richard's doctor at NYU wants him to consider hospice care since his cancer has grown rapidly in the last week. They believe it is past the point where it can be treated.

We are not sure what we will do yet. It is all very sad.

Love,
Barbara

Thursday October 27, 2011

Richard wanted me to send this update to all of you.

He has been able to breathe better since the old catheter in his right pleural space was replaced with a new one. .2 liters were drained yesterday and .45 liters today. A catheter may be inserted in his left pleural space tomorrow if it seems that fluid is continuing to accumulate there. 1.2 liters were drained in total on Tuesday and Wednesday. No fluid needed to be drained today.

An ultrasound of the abdomen this morning showed that there was not any obvious place to drain fluid to remove pressure in this area.

Over the last 24 hours, Richard's abdomen has become more bloated. An x-ray late this afternoon, showed a possible blockage in his intestine. This will be checked with additional tests on Friday. In the meantime, Richard is on intravenous feeding using a sodium chloride solution. Also, he has a tube inserted thru his nose into his stomach to remove food which has built up in his abdomen. This should make Richard more comfortable.

The medical team was concerned with Richard's continuing high potassium and low sodium levels. A kidney specialist today said this was caused by the cancer and that when Richard is allowed to eat again, he should limit his water intake, increase his protein intake and lower his potassium intake. If Richard feels thirsty, he suggested that Richard suck on a candy or eat an ice cube. He said neither Gatorade nor Ensure were good because of their high potassium content. Instead, he said Richard should drink Nepro, a supplement similar to Ensure but without the potassium.

Lastly, a palliative care doctor today recommended serorquel to calm Richard and make it easier to sleep and fentenal to make his breathing less labored. Fentenal is a synthetic version of morphine which is easier on the liver and kidneys and also does not leave one with a groggy feeling. We will see how this works tonight.

Because of these outstanding issues, Richard will unfortunately need to stay in the hospital over the weekend.

Through all of this, Richard has amazingly remained in reasonably good spirits.

Barbara

Photograph by Harold Geller

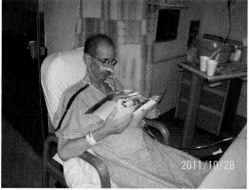
Photograph by Harold Geller

Saturday October 30, 2011

Richard is continuing to stabilize here at NYU Hospital.

Pleural Fluid:
The fluid in Richard's pleural space has stabilized. Left: 1200 ml were drained by gravity last Monday and Tuesday but since then, no more has accumulated. Right: A small amount of fluid has been drained each day from the right pleural space using a PleurX® catheter (.3, .2, .45, .36, .16 liters daily from Tuesday thru Saturday respectively). Fluid seems to be accumulating in this area at a lower rate then the approximately 1 liter/day that was drained thru most of October.

Partial Small Intestine blockage
Richard felt extremely bloated and was unable to eat or drink on Thursday. An x-ray, revealed a partial blockage of the small intestine caused by a tumor. As of Thursday evening, Richard has been put on a sodium chloride iv, given octretide intravenously every 12 hours to rest the bowel, and had a naso-gastric tube (NG tube) inserted thru his nose to his stomach to pump out undigested food that has backed up in his stomach. So far, he has passed gas, had 3 very small bowel movements, and developed some sounds in his bowels. The doctors said that if this progress continues, Richard may be able to move to a clear liquid diet on Monday and then gradually move to digestible food.

Electrolytes
Richard potassium level has been very high and his sodium has been low. As a result, fluid has been accumulating in Richard's 'third space' including development of edema in Richard's legs and feet. Over the

last few days, Richard's potassium level has dropped to 5.1 (3.6-5.2 normal range) and his sodium has risen to 135 (134-146 normal range). A kidney specialist is monitoring this.

Possible infection
Richard's white blood cell count is very high at 29.6 (3.7-11.4 normal range). The doctors say there is no clear evidence of infection but they would like to bring in an infectious disease specialist to do future checking. They are going to do blood and urine cultures today.

Sleeping
Richard continues to have trouble sleeping at night. He is now getting Seroquel (50 mg) before bed and Fentanyl (50mg) as a patch. Since Richard sometimes requests not to receive the medication, his doctors have asked that he consistently use it so they can see if the dosage is correct or if another drug needs to be prescribed.

Other
Richard's LDH count (a tumor marker) has changed from 1068 on 10/19 when Richard was taken off of the BRAF/MEK trial to 1414 on 10/29/11 and to 1164 on 10/30/11. The normal range is 313-618. Richard started the IPI/BRAF combo getting his first dose of IPI on Thursday 10/20/11 and restarted BRAF again on 10/24/11. I am hopeful that the combo IPI/BRAF drugs have some synergy and are influencing Richard's good results.

Richard has enjoyed watching sporting events on ESPN at the hospital. This afternoon, there is a Giants football game which he will watch.

Barbara

The New York Giants won that football game over the Miami Dolphins that day by a score of 20 to 17. The New York Giants went on to win the Super Bowl, defeating the New England Patriots 21 to 17. Unfortunately Richard B. Geller, a lifelong New York Giant football fan didn't get to see that happen.

My brother, Richard B. Geller, died on November 1, 2011, sometime after 1 PM in the afternoon at NYU Medical Center Hospital in New York City. He was 65 years old and to him his family and math was #1.